SCHIRMER BOOKS
THEATRE
MANUALS

SCHIRMER BOOKS
THEATRE
MANUALS

DIRECTING A PLAY

Michael McCaffery

Series editor: David Mayer

SCHIRMER BOOKS

Acknowledgements
The author and publisher gratefully acknowledge the help and assistance of the staff and students of the Royal Academy of Dramatic Art, London, in particular Adrienne Allen, Darren Clarke, Henrietta Garden, and Carl Picton, for their participation in the photographs taken by Michael Prior.

Photographs: Michael Prior pp.20–21, 25, 27–29, 41, 47, 51–53, 68, 72–78, 80, 83–85, 96–97, 100, 103, 113, 117; Regents Park Theatre p.63; Oxford Stage Company pp. 17, 23, 32, 55, 57, 64, 71, 87, 89, 109, 111.

Illustration: Jones, Sewell and Associates pp. 15, 22, 36, 44, 49, 58–62, 67, 93, 95. Miller, Craig and Cocking pp. 19, 22, 36, 92.

First American edition published in 1989 by Schirmer Books

A Division of Macmillan, Inc.

Copyright © 1988 by Phaidon Press Limited, Oxford 1988

Schirmer Books
A Division of Macmillan, Inc.
866 Third Avenue, New York, N. Y. 10022

First published in Great Britain by Phaidon Press Limited, Oxford

Library of Congress Catalog Card Number: 88-18167

Printed and bound in Singapore under co-ordination by C S Graphics Pte Ltd

printing number
1 2 3 4 5 6 7 8 9 10

Library of Congress Cataloging-in-Publication Data

McCaffery, Michael.
  Directing a play

  (Schirmer Books theatre manuals)
  Bibliography: p.
  Includes index.
  1. Theater – Production and direction.   I. Title.
II. Series.
PN2053.M32 1989   792'.0233   88-15830
ISBN 0-02-871342-7

ISBN 0-02-871341-9 (set)

Designed by Miller, Craig and Cocking, Woodstock

Contents

INTRODUCTION

Work in the theatre is always undertaken with a future performance in mind, but two artistic facts of life affect this work. One is that no one, no matter how naturally talented and accomplished, can invariably count on inspiration to solve a problem. The other fact is that time is the most precious of all theatrical commodities. The date of a first performance is an unalterable deadline, and that deadline, in turn, determines a whole sequence of earlier deadlines which must be met within the resources, not always ideal, that are available to the theatrical team.

These facts have been our starting-point in devising this series. Inspiration may be rare, but creativity, we suggest, can be supplemented by technique. Effective organization coupled with careful forward-planning can result in impressive productions. Experience has shown that good preparation will actually free the creative imagination and give it room to flourish.

This series has been designed to meet the needs of those working in the non-professional theatre, that is students and undergraduates, school teachers, and members of amateur dramatic and operatic societies. This is not an indication of the standards of the performances to be achieved; some amateur productions are quite outstanding. In fact some of the differences between the amateur and the professional are in the amateurs' favour: amateur groups can often call upon enormous resources for behind-the-scenes labour and the large casts that are so often out of reach of most professional companies. But non-

professionals are more likely to be limited by the amount of time, money, space and materials available. We recognize that you will be working with some or all of these advantages and restrictions, and we offer ways of looking at problems which will stimulate the imagination and produce solutions. The answers will then be yours, not ours.

Putting on a play is essentially teamwork, teamwork which depends upon the creativity of administrators and craftsmen, performers, directing staff and stage crews. The team can best thrive when responsibilities are shared and lines of communiciation are always open, direct and cordial. In recognition of these needs we have linked the books by planning charts and repeating themes looked at from different angles in order to emphasize that the best results are always achieved when skills are pooled.

Dozens of performances and hours of discussion lie behind these texts, and while we cannot claim to have covered every eventuality, we are confident that the approach outlined in the following pages will lead to productions that are successful, imaginative, and, above all, enjoyable for you, your colleagues, and your audiences.

David Mayer

Safety

Attention to safety is vitally important when you are putting on any production. When there is a procedure in this book where special care must be taken a safety flash *has been inserted in the margin.*

CHAPTER I

THE DIRECTOR'S ROLE

Throughout any theatrical production the director is pivotal to the success of the operation. You will be entrusted with the responsibility of making decisions which affect the artistic and often the financial welfare of the entire production. The stock image of an all-powerful, irrational but brilliant dictator is no longer appropriate, and the director who wants to direct merely because of the power involved will find it difficult to function at all in a production team. The importance of your position is recognized by the theatre structure in which you work and is reflected in the trust which colleagues place in you. You may win minor battles by steamrollering your decision through, but will quickly lose the goodwill which you need to survive when difficulties arise. The director is entrusted with identifying and selecting those elements of a play which will make for a successful production, and with choosing and guiding collaborators towards putting this into practice. More than anything, a director works *with* the production team and must develop flexibility of approach. Remember that levels of ability or achievement are not always uniform, so it is up to you always to be prepared and to be clear about what you want to achieve. Each member of the team makes an essential contribution to the overall product and it is the director's task to proportion and harness their abilities. One-man-bands seldom make good directors.

WHAT DOES THE DIRECTOR DO?

As director you will initiate, develop and co-ordinate all the work involved in a production. You will assess the play's demands on all members of the group and combine their contributions to make them into a satisfying whole.

You will work with actors, casting them for the parts, advising them on characterization and generally preparing them for public performance. You will be working with a designer to create an on-stage environment that will enhance the audience's enjoyment and understanding of the performance, and with back-stage workers to get the result you want.

You will be the creative and organizing centre of the whole business of putting on a play. You cannot be expert in everything but you must be able to gauge each group member's contribution and spot their weaknesses. A good director will recognize the strengths of the team and its limitations, and guide it to the most economical and creative results. Basic to this is clarity in your own mind about what you want. Above all, if you are to prepare the production for performance, you must prepare yourself.

WHAT QUALITIES DOES A DIRECTOR NEED?

When you read a play you must be able to see it as a piece of theatre. You must also be able to reduce a text to its working components, and this analysis is as important to the work as is inspiration. Regard inspiration as a useful – but sometimes dangerous – plus.

The ability to quantify, qualify and communicate the production needs of a text is vital. So is an interest in people and in their attachment to the theatre. This means *listening* to what they have to contribute. The director who *only tells* is likely to become frustrated and unpopular.

You must be flexible, especially when you work with non-professional or inexperienced colleagues. Also remember that while you must know what you want from them you have no right to demand it. Patience with others is important, for you and for them; it keeps the pressure off. Your production will succeed only through others' contributions, so you should value rather than take them for granted. If you lead well, your leadership will be accepted.

HOW IMPORTANT IS THE DIRECTOR?

The director is central to the whole project, and has responsibility and power. Use your power selfishly and you will lose the respect you need in tough situations. Maintain a visible presence. Spend time with your colleagues and take an interest in their work. They will appreciate your importance to it.

TIME AND THE DIRECTOR

Time is the most valuable item on your budget, and used badly it becomes your worst enemy. *You will never have too much time.* Whatever production schedule you work out it will never be long enough, so look at yours realistically. Relate the number of working sessions to the ground to be covered, and plan everything in detail beforehand. If you can control the time-factor you are on course for a successful production.

Pre-production Period

Function	Pre-rehearsal Period
Administrator	Check play available for performance. Check score available for performance. Negotiate royalty payments. Check venue available. Pre-production discussions with Director and Designers. Check licensing and permission, especially firearms. Check credit card registration. Gather programme material. Plan publicity. Announce auditions. Determine budget.
Director	Pre-production discussions. Conduct auditions – with choreographer and Musical Director. Announce casting. Announce and initiate rehearsal schedules.
Production Manager/ Technical Director	Pre-production budget meeting with Administration. Design meeting with Director, Designer and Stage Manager. Appoint Stage Manager and technical staff.
Stage Management	Attend design meeting and run auditions. Prepare prompt copy and provisional lists. Research with designer. Gather rehearsal props, furniture and set. Find a rehearsal space.
Scenic Design and Construction	Pre-production discussions. Model making: technical and working. Prepare drawings. Prepare prop drawings. Get Director's approval. Prepare castings and planning.
Lighting	Pre-production discussions. Read and re-read text. Research & Planning costume and scene.
Sound	Pre-production discussions. Read and re-read text. Prepare a selection of provisional tapes. Get Director's approval.
Music	Check availability of scores. Organize a rehearsal pianist. Audition singers. Agree rehearsal schedule with Director. Gather orchestra.,
Choreography Fights	Check rehearsal space. Organize rehearsal pianist. Audition dancers. Agree rehearsal schedule with Director.
Costume Design and Construction	Pre-production discussions. Costume research and drawing. Working drawings for wigs/hats/shoes. Fabric sampling. Costing and planning.

Function	Week 6	Week 5	Week 4	Week 3
Administration	Gather programme material. Display publicity material. Open booking if necessary.	Start press stories. Monitor publicity. Monitor bookings. Contact with rehearsals.	Recruit FOH staff if required. Invite critics.	Direct sell.
Director	Attend production meeting. ■ Discussions ■ Script cuts ■ Note running time.	Blocking rehearsal.	Business rehearsals. Rehearsal props introduced. Attend meetings. Listen to sound tape. Lighting meeting	Singers and dancers integrated. Reblocking. ■ Pianist present. Orchestral rehearsal.
Production Manager	Costing meetings with set, prop and costume makers. Production meeting. Problem solving and budget decisions.	Coordinating technical departments and budget control.		Progress meeting. Arrange for equipment h Liaison with venue.
Stage Management	Mark out and prepare rehearsal space. Note script changes. Attend production and props meetings.	Run rehearsal Prop, furniture and dressings search and making. Liaison with all departments.		Attend progress meeting. Arrange sound and lightin, meetings for director
Scenic design and construction	Meetings and planning with technical director. ■ Attend read through Call for actors, staff and workshop. Scenic construction and propmaking.	Liaison with SM and workshop. ■ Buy soft furnishings.	■ Choose hire furniture and scene painting.	Drawings for new props. Alterations as necessary.
Costume design and construction make up	Attend first rehearsal.	Artwork and photography for projection. ■ Construction special lighting affects.	Preliminary fittings.	
Lighting	Attend production meeting. Keep in contact rehearsals – SM/Director/Designer. Liaison with Director and Designer		■ Check stock.	Attend rehearsal and run through.
Sound	Attend production meeting. Basic provisional tape in rehearsal.	Research and planning. ■ Check stock and buy in tapes, effects records, etc. Meeting with director.	Prepare effects tapes. Sound meetings with director.	Record special effects. Record hire effects with actors. ■ Design sound rig. ■ Hire equipment.
Music	Singing rehearsals. Music rehearsals.			Singers join main rehearsal
Choreography and fights	Dancing rehearsals. Fight rehearsals.		Hire weapons with SM.	Fights choreographed. Dancers join main rehearsa

Week 2	Day 7	Day 6	Day 5	Day 4	Day 3	Day 2	Day 1
vite press to hotocall.	Check Box. Engage FOH staff. ■ Ushers. ■ Sales. ■ Box Office.	Train FOH staff. Arrange FOH displays. Print programmes.				Photo call.	
olish rehearsal. Fights in rehearsal. eet to discuss lighting. eet with sound dept, to heck final FX.	Introduce performance props.		Run through	Attend lighting and sound plotting sessions.	Attend technical rehearsal and give notes.	Photo call, dress rehearsal give notes.	Final dress rehearsal and gives notes.
ark up production chedule. Arrange transport nd staff for the get in/fit up nd show staff.	Supervise get in and fit up as per production schedule	Continue fit up as per schedule (+ LX main rig).	Continue as per schedule. Possible fire inspection	Supervise schedule. (LX and sound plotting sessions).	Attend technical rehearsal.	Supervise technical work on stage. Attend dress rehearsal.	Supervise technical work on stage. Attend final dress rehearsal.
rrange lighting designer to ee an early run through. Director to listen to sound ape. Prepare setting lists nd cue sheets.	Run rehearsals. Team attend run through. Finalize setting lists, cue sheets	Help fit up paint etc. Find props adjustments.	Team help more out of rehearsal rooms to venue.	Dress the set Set the props. Attend LX and sound plotting sessions.	Possible scene change rehearsal. Run technical rehearsal.	Run Dress rehearsal. Attend Director's note session.	Run final dress rehearsal.
rop meetings to check all rops. Attend Lighting Discussion.	Fit up and painting as per production.	Continue fit up and painting as per production schedule.	Fit up and paint end texture as per schedule.	Attend lighting session and LX plotting. Dress the set.	Attend technical rehearsal.	Attend photo call. Attend dress rehearsal.	Technical work as necessary. Attend dress rehearsal.
	Check costumes, Check wigs arrived.	Get in for costumes. Costumes to dressing rooms.	Attend run through.	Attend run through Check make up.	Attend technical rehearsal. Check make up under lights.		
	Finalize copy lighting design. Preliminary rigging. Hired equipment arrives.	Lighting rigging.	Focusing of lighting.	Lighting session plotting.	Technical rehearsal.	Dress rehearsal. Attend notes sessions. Technical work on stage.	Final dress rehearsal. Technical work on stage.
Preparation of final tapes. ■ Rehearse live sound mixing – mini-tech. Director to hear tape.	Hired equipment arrives. Mini sound tech with orchestra.	Sound rigging.	Attend run through.	Sound plotting rework tapes.	Technical rehearsal. Rework tapes.	Dress rehearsal. Rework tapes. Attend notes session.	Final dress rehearsal. Attend notes session.
Musicians rehearse with sound reinforcement if necessary.				Rehearsal for orchestra and cast.	Technical rehearsal, piano only.	Dress rehearsal with orchestra.	
Fights join main rehearsal.		Choreographer present as needed.					

The Run and Post Production

Function	The Run	Post Production
Administrator	Show reports to Director. FOH staff checks. Monitor sales. Liaise with Stage Manager.	File prompt script and production paperwork. Collect scripts. Pay accounts.
Director	Note running times. Director's notes to cast. Warnings and encouragement before performance. Keep contact with SM for problems.	File director's script. Compile report on production and contact list for cast or production team.
Production Manager	Work on budget accounts with Administration. Check orchestra pit.	Arrange transport and staff for get-out. Supervise get-out and storage of any stock set. Supervise returns of hired/borrowed equipment. Final work on accounts with Administration return scores.
Stage Management	Run shows as per prompt script, running lists, etc. Check set, props, furniture settings. Supervise understudy rehearsals. Show reports.	Get out props, dressings and furniture. Supervise return of hired and borrowed items and stock to stores. Assemble prompt script and all lists, plots, etc. for the show and file with Administration.
Scenic Design and Construction		Sort out scenic stock to keep with Production Manager.
Lighting	Check performances crew present. Check equipment pre-performance. Run Show.	Dismantle and store lighting equipment. Return hired equipment. File lighting plot.
Sound	Check performances crew present. Check equipment pre-performance. Run Show.	Dismantle and store sound equipment. Store tapes and catalogue for future. Return hired equipment.
Costume Design		Cleaning and storage of costumes. File costume Bible.

THE TEAM

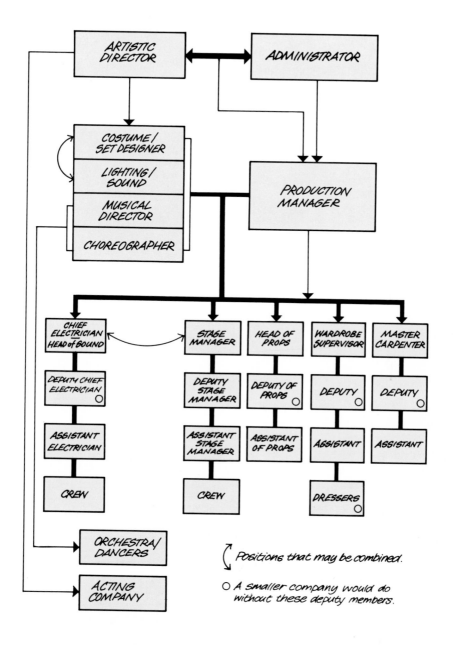

- ARTISTIC DIRECTOR
- ADMINISTRATOR
- COSTUME / SET DESIGNER
- LIGHTING / SOUND
- MUSICAL DIRECTOR
- CHOREOGRAPHER
- PRODUCTION MANAGER
- CHIEF ELECTRICIAN HEAD of SOUND
- STAGE MANAGER
- HEAD OF PROPS
- WARDROBE SUPERVISOR
- MASTER CARPENTER
- DEPUTY CHIEF ELECTRICIAN
- DEPUTY STAGE MANAGER
- DEPUTY OF PROPS
- DEPUTY
- DEPUTY
- ASSISTANT ELECTRICIAN
- ASSISTANT STAGE MANAGER
- ASSISTANT OF PROPS
- ASSISTANT
- ASSISTANT
- CREW
- CREW
- DRESSERS
- ORCHESTRA / DANCERS
- ACTING COMPANY

Positions that may be combined.

○ A smaller company would do without these deputy members.

13

CHAPTER 2

CHOOSING A PRODUCTION

Explore all areas in your search for a script. Above all be sure that the final choice is one that you want to direct, that your group can perform, and that will draw an audience.

HOW IMPORTANT IS YOUR CHOICE?

A production is only as good as its director can make it, and what works for one may not for another. Your abilities will be on trial, so ensure your chosen play is within them.

Your script choice will affect everyone involved in its production, and in the often tough times ahead you will need sound basic material to help you convince colleagues that the work is worthwhile and getting somewhere. So you too must be convinced.

HOW ABOUT COPYRIGHT?

Most plays are subject to some kind of copyright, and you must get performance rights *before rehearsal*. Not to do so is illegal – and can be expensive. Copyright exists in

✳ YOUR SEARCH STARTS HERE

PLAY TYPE	LIBRARY	COLLEAGUE	BOOKSHOP	PUBLISHER	AGENT	PERF. COMPANY	COPYRIGHT LIBRARY
KNOWN CLASSICS	1 ✳ →	✳ →	✳ →	✳ →		✳ →	✳
LESSER KNOWN CLASSICS	1 ✳ →	✳ →	✳ →			✳ →	✳
FOREIGN LANGUAGE CLASSICS	✳ →	✳ →	1 ✳ →	✳ ····		····	✳
FOREIGN LANGUAGE NEW			1 ✳ →		✳ →	✳ →	✳
WELL KNOWN PLAYS CONTEMPORARY	✳ ←		1 ✳ →	✳ →	✳ →		✳
NEW WRITING			(✳)	(✳)	✳ ←	1 ✳	
MUSICALS	✳			1 ✳	1 ✳		✳

EXCELLENT ──── GOOD ──── FAIR ──── POOR ──── BAD

the United Kingdom on *all* plays whose authors are still living or who have been dead for less than fifty years. In the United States copyright is granted for twenty-five years from the first showing and is subsequently renewable. With music-theatre works, there are variants which allow copyright to be maintained beyond these periods by publishers.

WHO MAKES THE CHOICE?

So much relies on the right choice of play that many theatre companies, reluctant to leave it to one person, have a reading or selection committee, which can read more plays than a lone director and can advise on problems that particular works may present. (Of course, if you direct a play chosen by a majority vote you can, if you later find yourself its sole defender, point out that others wanted it too.)

But, however a play is selected, the *final* choice – whether you will direct or not – is yours.

WHO FORMS A READING COMMITTEE?

A reading committee should comprise representatives of all the departments to be involved in the production – director, stage manager, wardrobe supervisor, administrator, actors and someone who understands stage design, though not necessarily your designer. All should read the scripts, both from a general point of view and from their specialist ones. Without a reading committee the director must do all this.

First step is to understand the play. Take time to read it thoroughly.

WHAT TO LOOK FOR IN A SCRIPT?

A script *must interest you*. You must *want to direct it*. Next, consider how well you and your group can meet the demands it will make. Be realistic here or you may lead your team into artistic and financial failure – after a miserable production period with people working hard but knowing themselves unequal to the job. Check, too, that you can meet any special demands the script makes for music, dance, fights or special effects. All need *time, space, money and skills*.

The next thing is *casting*. You need not have as many actors as the play has roles but you must be able to cast with those that you do have, *and the roles must be within their range*. Parts are often harder to play than directors realize, so be cautious when you read with casting in mind.

Once certain that the play is within your scope, check that it is available for performance and that scripts are cheap and easy to get. Photocopies are illegal and often cost more than publishers' copies.

CHECKLIST

* What kind of audience do we have?
* What kind of audience do we want?
* Will regular members want to come?
* Does the play have local or topical interest?
* Is the show popular?
* When was the show last done and how well?
* How hard will we have to sell it?
* Can we afford special publicity?
* Will cast members be useful in selling?
* Do we usually sell through cast members?
* How much will our tickets cost?

Have you thought about how to sell this show?

CAN WE FIND AN AUDIENCE?

Though often the last thing in a director's mind, a production's audience-pulling power needs careful thought. Not only does your group's financial success – even its survival – depend on a popular choice, you will all be working hard, perhaps for months, and even the highest artistic achievement will not compensate for a poor audience. Indeed, the better the production the more people you will want to see it!

Even well-known plays can do badly at the box-office. Ask the licensing agent when yours was last done in the area, also, if there is a film version, when it was last shown locally. A recent film of your play can still leave you an agonizing decision. The success of another version can breed success for a successor – or it can sate people's interest in the work.

Given all this, remember that a quality production will be your big selling point. If *you* see a script as one that you and your team can do well, you must persuade the others that, however unfamiliar, it is worth doing and selling. You should take marketing and sales of seats into your overall strategy at this stage and be prepared to get involved in that side of things too.

CHAPTER 3

PREPARATION

This is the director's most important period, providing a basis for all the work to be done by the group. It can be very enjoyable and you should make the most of it. Don't feel guilty about being answerable only to yourself. The period equips you for all your pre-production work. It should give you growing confidence and flexibility in the actual production work. Try to be methodical. Don't try to do everything at once. Let things develop. Allow yourself as much time as possible – but keep it structured.

IS PREPARATION NECESSARY?

The director's work before rehearsals start is essential. It ensures that the various departments are briefed well in advance so as to be ready for performance at the same time as the actors, and also that they will be ready to take the load off the director when, in rehearsal, the actors naturally take priority. The more you do now the less trouble you will have later.

HOW IS A SCRIPT PREPARED?

The work comes under three headings: *Interpretation*, *Technical Requirements*, and *Administration*. These are interlinked and will become interdependent, but try to keep them separate in the early stages. Put them together only when you feel that you control all the elements of each.

PROBLEM	RESEARCH AT
LANGUAGE	O.E.D. CHAMBERS DICTIONARY
HISTORY	PUBLIC LIBRARY
LOCAL HISTORY	PUBLIC LIBRARY REFERENCE ARCHIVES COLLECTION
BIOGRAPHY	NATIONAL DICTIONARY OF BIOGRAPHY LIBRARIES
MUSIC	DICTIONARY OF MUSIC AND MUSICIANS
MUSIC SOURCES	BBC CATALOGUE OF PRINTED MUSIC
SCIENCE	ENCYCLOPAEDIA BRITANNICA
MYTHOLOGY	DICTIONARY OF THE ANCIENT WORLD
FOLKLORE & CULTURE	VARIOUS LIBRARY REFERENCES

WHEN YOU DON'T UNDERSTAND

The director *must* understand the whole play. However intricate your conception of the work your success depends on your ability to communicate it to – and eventually through – the actors from moment to moment. When there are things you do not understand admit them, and discuss the play with friends and colleagues, even those not involved. Classical and period plays often raise problems of understanding due to social or political change, affecting our understanding of characters and their motivation, so try to grasp what the play meant in its own time. Where a work seems illogical or inconsistent re-read it from the angle of the character or event that confuses you – always remember that fiction does not operate in the same way as observable fact. Many plays have implausible or unexplained incidents. These may be pointers to style.

HOW USEFUL IS RESEARCH?

Many directors dismiss research, saying that the play should speak for itself and that, as audiences will not understand the references, background detail is not important. This approach often produces superficial and uninteresting theatre. Perhaps more than any other form theatre uses the world in which – and for which – it is written as material for its subjects. The more remote that world the more important is the research that can 'open' the play to director, designer, actors and audience. Research is useless only when a director uses it to score points off colleagues or to defend shaky production ideas. Encourage all your colleagues to do research and to share their findings with each other. Extend it to people and customs rather than limiting it to period details of objects and dress styles. The more you know, the more you are in control.

Time, space and actors are theatre's vital components. Give them priority in planning and budgeting.

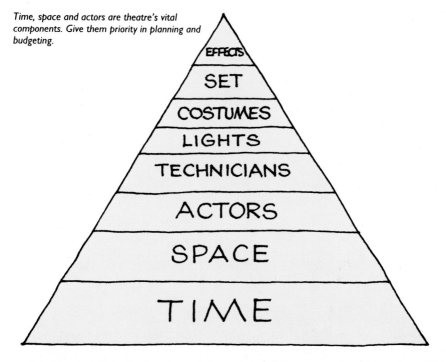

PREPARING A SCRIPT FOR PRODUCTION

Read the script thoroughly, and as often as you need to know precisely *what happens*, *where it happens*, *when it happens* and *who is involved in it*. If music is involved familiarize yourself thoroughly with it by listening to recordings or, if none are to be had, get the printed music and work with that. If you don't read music get a pianist friend to record it for you – though this can be expensive and must be done without breaking copyright laws.

When you feel yourself in control of the material read the script again and try to envisage, however sketchily, the way the action will unfold on stage. Avoid any interpretation of the text that you know to be beyond your group's resources. As you read ask yourself questions like:

■ where is this scene set?
A new location, or is the
action continuous?
■ is a scene change required?
lighting change? is there
link music?
■ where does the actor enter
on the stage? where has the
character come from? what has
happened since you last saw
the character?

■ what does the character look
like? costume or make-up change?
special effect?
■ what do viewers know at this
point that they didn't know
earlier?
■ why is this scene in the play?
action? mood? how does it relate
to what happens elsewhere in
the script?

Keep detailed notes throughout your work on the script. Later there will be much to think about and memory may not be reliable. Notes will remind you *why* you wanted something as well as what it was, so keep them lucid and legible.

Buy *two* copies of the play and paste the pages – for example, page 1 from one and page 2 from the other – into a large-format notebook, leaving ample space round the printed text and blank facing pages for longer notes, sketches or outlines of moves. This 'production copy' will make sense mainly to you, but it is the starting point of all the work you will do with your colleagues. Early ideas often find their way into final production, so *record* yours.

WHAT DOES THE PLAY NEED?

Different plays require different things of any group presenting them, but an experienced director develops formulas that help in spotting particular problems in advance. The first-time director has no experience to call on for such guidance, so it is important that you anticipate from the script alone what will be needed for successful presentation and what may obstruct it.

The basic elements of any theatre work are: **time, space, actors, technicians, settings, costumes, lights**, and **effects**. You may dispense with or modify some of these without impoverishing your production – costumes, say, are not always necessary – but you must consider the work from each of these aspects to understand its overall needs.

The **time** you will need to rehearse the play depends on how long it is. Once familiar with it, read it aloud, timing each scene – but not at one sitting; fatigue will incline you to speed up or slow down. Compare the time-length of the play with your available rehearsal time. Remembering that you will be rehearsing for a set number of hours each week, try to decide how many hours you will need for adequate rehearsal. If you do not have enough time ask for more. As noted above, there is never too much time.

The **actors** available will also affect the rehearsal time. *Inexperienced actors need longer in rehearsal than others.* Look at how much learning each actor will have to do and ensure that no one you cast will have learning problems. If the play makes specific demands – of height, weight, swiftness of movement – remember these when deciding the kind of performers you will need. Similarly, if the play demands actors of a particular type – good comedians, perhaps, or actors of power or subtlety – make sure

they are available. You cannot get the right performance out of the wrong actor. Finally be sure that *all* the actors you want to cast will be available whenever you want them.

Every production needs adequate **technicians**, the more complex the project the more of them. Willing hands are vital, but so is experience. Arrange with your production manager that each group is led and its work co-ordinated by an experienced person. Remember, too, that any sophisticated or unusual technical effects need special equipment as well as skilled operators. Make sure that you have both.

Settings and **costumes** are vital parts of a production, and while you may decide to ignore the author's ideas about these, some sort of setting and special clothes will be needed if you are to create the effect you envisage. If you have not yet thought about what the actors will wear and what their environment will be you should go back to the script and make up your mind before going further.

Lighting and **special effects** will be the last things to appear in rehearsal, but consider them from the start. They will occupy many people in your group for weeks ahead, so be clear about what you want to see and take advice on how it can be achieved. All theatre work has lighting and special-effects requirements. Read the script closely to discover their precise nature – including the dialogue, for the actors' words are as important as the stage directions here. Many classical plays have no stage directions, but the actors' speeches indicate specific structures, effects or atmosphere on stage. Consider, for example, the various things said about, and done with, Juliet's tomb before deciding how to stage Act 5 of *Romeo and Juliet*.

Pre-planning and co-ordinating are essential. The planning charts in this book are here to assist you in this work.

ENTRANCES AND EXITS

The commonest questions from an actor are 'Where do I enter?' and 'How do I get off?'. The answers may be obvious to you but not to the player, and the audience will get confused if you have not plotted the play with the set's external geography in mind.

The visible space in which a play takes place is related through action and dialogue to notional offstage space invisible to the audience. Thus it is important for clarity that the actors' use of particular exits and entrances be consistent. Decide from the script what spaces notionally lie beyond the playing space. Each door must lead somewhere. Be clear about where each of these spaces is and what it means to the viewer. Farces, particularly, depend on offstage spaces being used consistently and logically throughout. Be sure to have a good reason for bringing characters back by different entrances from the ones by which they left. Too many doors and entrances are as destructive as too few. Also remember that all important entrances must be visible from out in front.

HOW MANY LEVELS?

Most playing spaces are flat, but you may want to change this for various reasons – the simplest being to improve the audience's view of the stage. Most halls and venues offer a workable situation which you can, with the help of your designer, turn into a playing space.

You may want to vary the levels, especially for a musical or opera, to improve chorus sightlines on the conductor and enhance sound quality, or as a production point expressing relationships between characters. Rostra of various heights offer the simplest solution and a raked stage gives a more unified and satisfactory stage picture, but either are costly to build. Be sure that such variants are essential before asking for them.

Before preparing the visual aspect of your production go with your stage or technical manager to the play's venue. Doubtless you will already have some basic staging ideas, and it is better to check the venue's possibilities early than to create an imaginary set of requirements and be disappointed later.

The unraked stage: the front actor enjoys total prominence; those upstage lose stature and visibility while those behind the front row are lost.

The raked stage: this improves visibility and upstage actors' stature.

*Here every actor's performance is visible,
contributing to the scene.*

DIRECTOR AND DESIGNER

Your first and most enduring partnership as director will be with your designer. Together you will determine the visual approach to the production, briefing and working with the people who create the physical objects needed for realizing the play on stage and combining them in a coherent and pleasing end product.

The relationship between director and designer is close, and can be very fulfilling or frustrating and unproductive. It should be approached in the knowledge that neither of you can function without the other, and that you are there to help each other. You may, like some directors, start with the idea that you know just what you want and need no designer. This may sometimes be true up to a point, but in that case it is wiser to choose a designer who can work with you on that basis rather than not use one at all.

The designer takes care of the entire visual aspect of the production and so must be available for consultation during the preparation of all its visual content.

A good director will want to be in the rehearsal room with the cast as much as possible, but it is unfair to expect good co-operative work from the technical members of the group without adequate consultation. Your designer will do this – and with more focus and concentration than you could bring to it.

Ideally you and your designer should fuel each other creatively, help each other to greater understanding of the script with each session. If you do not like what a designer is doing you should say so at once rather than waste precious time. Delay here can also diminish a designer's interest in your overall concept and his or her trust in your ability to do the play.

It is possible that a designer may not like you or your work, in which case you must address the problem together, preferably without confrontation. Be sure that you are not the problem before you decide that a designer is unsatisfactory. Mutual trust between you is essential, and you should be able to enjoy the creative relationship, not feel threatened by it.

WHAT THE DESIGNER NEEDS TO KNOW

- ☑ WHAT YOU THINK THE WORK IS ABOUT
- ☑ ITS PRINCIPAL ACTION
- ☑ THE DEMANDS IT MAKES ON STAGING
  - – HOW MANY SETS
  - – HOW MANY ENTRANCES
  - – HOW MANY LEVELS
  - – ANY SPECIAL EFFECTS
- ☑ HOW MANY ACTORS
- ☑ HOW MANY COSTUMES
- ☑ OVERALL MOOD AND ATMOSPHERE
- ☑ PERIOD
- ☑ STYLE OF PRODUCTION
- ☑ OVERALL EFFECT YOU WANT

THE WORKING RELATIONSHIP

Your work with the designer has three basic phases. Together you will explore the script and eventually arrive at a design for the production that is satisfying, aesthetically pleasing, and financially practicable. When the designer has made drawings and models you will together communicate your needs to the various technical people, and discuss any compromises that may have to be made *throughout* the working period.

During the rehearsal period try to see your designer often. Keep in touch at a personal level rather than just at production meetings or in public.

Finally you will work together in assembling the production on stage, polishing it through technical rehearsals and dress rehearsals. At this stage *listen closely to your designer*. The tangible product of all the group's work is now before you and both of you want a success. Your say will be final, but do not use your power arbitrarily. Try to see what the designer sees.

Use the model box to investigate, and even solve, production problems.

BRIEFING THE DESIGNER

Make sure that the designer gets a copy of the script – in the edition that will be used throughout production – well before your first meeting, when he or she will probably already have some ideas on style and presentation. But the designer cannot do a satisfactory job without your clear guidance on how you envisage the production. Start by simply discussing the script, how each of you sees it and would like it to be staged. This first meeting can be informal and discursive, but later ones should look at specific matters and pursue clear lines of investigation.

MEETING STAGE	WHAT HAPPENS	WHAT NEXT
1.	BASIC APPROACH · CONTENT AND STYLE · WHAT HAPPENS WHAT IS NEEDED · HOW IT MIGHT BE ACHIEVED · VENUE · PEOPLE·RESOURCES SPECIFIC DEMANDS	DESIGNER – Makes sketches and models. DIRECTOR – Reads play with designer's ideas in mind.
2.	DESIGNER PRESENTS PRELIMINARY SKETCHES AND ROUGH MODEL IDEAS · FEASIBILITY & SUITABILITY DISCUSSED · NEW IDEAS INTRODUCED – PRESENT CONCEPT ADOPTED OR ABANDONED	DESIGNER – rethinks or continues work. Prepares next meeting. DIRECTOR – Continues work on text to see play in design context.
3.	COLOUR MODEL PRESENTED FEASIBILITY AND NEW IDEAS DISCUSSED · SPECIFIC PROBLEMS IN STAGING BROUGHT UP BY DIRECTOR & SOLUTIONS SOUGHT · COSTUMES DISCUSSED IN MORE DETAIL	DESIGNER – works on staging problems – finishes models & gets costumes sketches ready. DIRECTOR – continues work concentrating on props.
4.	FINISHED MODEL PRESENTED AND COSTUME DESIGNS DISCUSSED AND APPROVED · PROPS LIST COMPLETED AND DISCUSSED	DESIGNER – continues to finish for presentation and design props. DIRECTOR – plans the production finally.
5.	PRESENTATION TO PRODUCTION MANAGER FOR FINAL COSTING · LIGHTING DESIGN PRESENT	DESIGNER – makes adaptations and prepares for build/make. DIRECTOR – available to designer if adaptations needed and work with S.M. for rehearsal.

Ensure that you both have the time you need
between the various stages.

THE DESIGNER IN REHEARSALS

Directors and designers sometimes part company during rehearsals, to meet again at the technical rehearsals with different ideas of what they are aiming for. Your designer should be actively involved in rehearsals. Particular moves and effects can be properly realized only by means of specially adjusted props and costumes, and the designer must understand what you are trying to achieve before any designs can be made. Invite the designer to important rehearsals and encourage visits. The cast will like to meet the person responsible for their appearance and you will have an informed, sympathetic but objective appraisal of your efforts so far. You will probably become protective of your work, but it is in everyone's interest to give a designer – and any other production team members – access to rehearsals when they need it.

Actors must work with what the designer invents, so the designer must explain how it works.

THE PRODUCTION TEAM

Every production needs a basic production team to ensure that work is completed on schedule and within budget. The team comprises: *the director, designer, production manager, lighting designer* or *chief electrician, stage manager* and *deputy stage manager, wardrobe supervisor, set builder, property maker* and, when relevant, *musical director.* The production team should meet early in the planning stage, then regularly thereafter. The meetings should be structured enough not to waste the time of individual members while dealing with all relevant production topics.

PRODUCTION MANAGERS

The production manager is responsible for co-ordinating and supervising all areas of scheduling, budgeting and the carrying out of work on a production. It can be a thankless job. Too often a production manager will ask for compromises, will seem to be saying 'no', and will tell you why something cannot be done. At such times remember that he or she is trying for the best possible results within available resources of time, money and skill. A production manager liaises between all the personnel involved and must be free to communicate with them all.

BRIEFING THE PRODUCTION MANAGER

From the earliest moment the production manager must be briefed on every detail of the production, then kept fully informed of any changes in emphasis or intention that emerge at any stage. When you have met the designer and formulated a basic approach, meet the production manager, preferably with the designer, and explain as much as you know about the overall shape and intention of the production. No detail is too small. Do not shirk mentioning ambitious or unusual ideas; at some point they will be important to you, and the production manager must be able to gauge your priorities in the production. Briefly, the more open and honest a director is with all colleagues the easier things will be for everyone concerned.

CHAPTER 4

THE BUDGET

However modest, your production must have a budget that reflects accurately how much money is needed to present the work to standards acceptable to you, your group and your audience without costing more than you can make from performances. Working to a budget is a crucial discipline, and not to do so may ruin your organization. Overspending in any area must be matched by economies in others or by generating more funds. Be clear about your priorities so that the production manager can cope with any unavoidable changes.

WHY BUDGET?

The budget ensures that each area of the production has enough money to do its job properly. As well as restricting spending in certain areas it provides for spending which you may not think necessary. In a voluntary group *only* the personnel are free, though even here there are hidden costs – working space, lighting and tools, refreshments, expenses incurred by the 'unsocial' hours that theatre work often entails. If you make some provision for these, however small, you will have a happier team.

Every budget must take account of the possible income from the audience, but *do not work back from that*. Calculate what the production will cost and see how you can meet it. If you cannot meet it re-think your production values rather than doing a cut-rate version. Cheap theatre cannot be disguised, but economical theatre is much better than extravagant theatre.

WHO DECIDES THE BUDGET?

The director, production manager and designer meet and discuss the financial needs of the work. The production manager, or administration, costs each item and compares the total with projected total income from the production. This includes not only ticket sales but also profits on programmes and refreshments, fund-raising activities and donations. The two totals must balance, and the director must co-operate in seeing that they do.

WHO MANAGES THE BUDGET?

The production manager controls the budget, and both director and designer must follow any spending instructions. It is dangerous to seek extra spending behind the production manager's back, no matter how little or how necessary you believe it to be. Remember that the success of your production depends as much on making the books balance, and it is very difficult to make money out of theatrical ventures, especially those with short runs. It is extremely unlikely that you will cover any unbudgeted costs at the box-office, but any group must deal with overspending – and that may mean using members' own money.

STICKING TO THE BUDGET

Start off at the initial planning stage, with realistic costing and no hidden or undisclosed costs. Figures arrived at must reflect the *real* costs of items to which they refer. If the director or designer conceals an idea the production manager is entitled to refuse to execute it when it comes up. Avoid surprise items and *do not guess* at the price of anything, especially materials. Suppliers will not donate or undersell stock. Do not assume 100 per cent attendance at any performance. A given production will draw only a certain type of audience, so you must be realistic about the drawing-power of yours.

Finally – heed the production manager's advice on agreed spending. If you need more ask for it, but remember that it will mean economies elsewhere. Forward planning is very important. The earlier you know your needs the more time you have to shop round – or to invent less expensive means of realizing them.

CHANGING PRIORITIES

Every theatre production changes emphasis between initial planning and final performance, and any material change this prompts – in costume, scenery, lighting, sound, music – means a budget shift. Discuss it with the production manager at once. Ask for what you want – but be ready to accept a refusal.

BUDGET

Circulation: Dir/Des/PM/SM/
Props/Tech

PRODUCTION ....
DATE ....

BUDGET   TO DATE

EXPENDITURE

Administration costs
  Stationery   ......
  Photocopying   ......
  Postage   ......
  Insurance   ......
  Telephone   ......
  Bank charges   ......
  Audit fee   ......

Venue costs
  Hire fee   ......
  Display costs   ......
  Publicity contra   ......
  Staff contra   ......

Marketing costs
  Design costs   ......
  Posters   ......
  Leaflets   ......
  Other print   ......
  Newspapers   ......
  Postage   ......
  Merchandising   ......
  Reserve

Production costs
  Fees (Director   ......
       (Designer   ......
       (Other   ......
  Set   ......
  Costumes   ......
  Wigs   ......
  Make up   ......
  Props   ......
  Furniture   ......
  Weapons   ......
  Transport   ......
  Lighting/sound   ......
  Musical instruments/scores ......
  Hire of rehearsal rooms   ......
  Licences/royalties/   ......
       Scripts

Total expenditure

SUPPOSE WE OVERSPEND?

Your aim must be to *avoid overspending*, but sometimes external factors can unexpectedly bump up costs, particularly the costs of venues, publicity, and other commercial areas.

The production manager will scrutinize all bills and accounts as they come in and will keep you informed of the situation. Any overspending will affect your production, as you will have to economize elsewhere to avoid an overall deficit. Be flexible and adaptable in this situation. Part of your creative job is to think up alternatives and expedients. When confronted with a spending crisis take all the advice you can get, especially from more experienced colleagues, who may know cheaper ways to get the effect you want. The very last resort is to consider paying for something privately. This means that financial catastrophe is looming, and that instead of trying to get things right you are working beyond your means.

Make sure at the less hectic planning stage that your ideas are genuinely feasible – or find alternatives to them. Decisions made later will be made under pressure, and may not be good ones. If you suspect that serious all-round overspending is likely you must tell your board of managers and let them solve the problem.

CHAPTER 5

PRE-REHEARSAL WORK

With budget and designs organized you can get on with your own preparation. When rehearsals start you must be able to direct and support any situation, so prepare yourself in advance to deal with any likely problem. Work in detail on the precise acting requirements of the play, on how you will cast and rehearse the production and on how you mean to approach the rehearsals. You must be quite clear about what you want to do and how you will set about doing it. Too many directors take short cuts at this stage. This is your last private time with the play, so enjoy it.

THE DIRECTOR BEFORE REHEARSALS

Read through the play again. You now know how the sets and costumes will look, what special effects you can include and roughly what shape the production will take. Visualize each scene in the context that you and the designer have created for it, with particular attention to the demands that it will make on the actors. Decide how many actors – and what kind – you will need.

Draw up an outline rehearsal schedule to help you budget the available time against the play's various demands. Work out, from your understanding of the production, the number and size of rehearsal rooms you will need. You can also use this period to get to know the play intimately, to grasp the author's intention in each scene so that you will be able to guide your company through the work. You do not have to be perfect,

but a director's lack of preparation soon shows, and loses the confidence of the cast.

PRE-REHEARSAL TASKS
CHOOSE PLAY
FIX REHEARSAL & SHOW DATES
READ PLAY MANY TIMES
FIX BUDGET
DECIDE STYLE & APPROACH
BRIEF DESIGNER
FINAL DESIGN WORK
CASTING
COSTING & APPROVAL OF DESIGN
FINAL PREPARATION
FIRST REHEARSAL

HOW MANY ACTORS?

Some plays demand as many actors as they have parts, and any attempt to reduce the number will result in confused storylines. But classical plays are notorious for their huge lists of characters and it is usually possible – even preferable – to mount such productions with the minimum number of actors needed to put it on satisfactorily. There is an honourable tradition of small-cast classical productions, and many actors enjoy the challenge of playing more than one role. It is crucial, though, that the actors be of equal ability.

An imaginative director with good actors can overcome the minuses. A poor cast under an uninspired director can throw away the pluses. Think carefully before you decide!

SMALL CAST PLUSES

Fewer actors produce a more concentrated rehearsal atmosphere

'Ensemble' playing is more likely

Higher acting standards may be aimed at

The director's concepts can be reinforced

Intimacy and detail can be better achieved

Stylistic unity in the acting is more feasible

Visual unity is more easily achieved

SMALL CAST MINUSES

More rehearsals per actor are needed, meaning high availability

Poor actors stand out more

Storylines suffer unless actors delineate different characters clearly

Crowd scenes need very imaginative treatment to be convincing

Acting may lack variety and contrast

Individual moments may suffer in context

Consider these points when deciding on the size of your cast.

ONE PART, ONE ACTOR

A big cast on stage can be exciting, but more people produce more problems and few big-cast plays benefit from a full complement of actors unless they are highly enthusiastic – and highly available. Large-scale productions are expensive too: thirty actors will need thirty costumes. But some parts can be doubled – played by the same actor.

Some actors hate doubling and prefer even a small single role. Others like to be kept busy, exercising their skills on the portrayal of contrasting characters. One-part-one-actor is best for a play in which the storyline is paramount, but when character and atmosphere are more important doubling can be interesting and very rewarding.

HOW TO DOUBLE YOUR ACTORS

If you want your doubling to work well you must bear some practical points in mind:

Do not put actors in different roles in consecutive scenes. They need time to adjust and to make costume changes if they are to give a relaxed performance. The audience needs some adjustment time too.

Split the play into 'French scenes' – begin a new scene each time a character enters. Go back to scene I for each new act to avoid unwieldy numbers.

Draw up a chart that tells you which characters are in each scene. This will show you which ones could be doubled, which ones could not, and how far apart their entrances must be. It will also enable you to determine, in turn, how big a cast you need to perform the play adequately. Try to classify characters in order of importance. Mark leading roles A, less important ones B, and so on down to an E or F grading. Only in very special circumstances should you double As or Bs. The demands of leading and secondary roles are such that doubling can exhaust the actors and tax the audience's credulity.

CHARACTER FREQUENCY CHART

	PROLOGUE	ACT 1 Sc 1 Peachum's Parlour	Sc 2 Stable	Sc 3 Peachum's	ACT ii Sc 4 Macheath's	Sc 4 Same	Sc 5 Whore House	Sc 6 Police Station	Act III Peachum's	Sc 7 Same	Sc 8 Lady's cell	Sc 9 Death cell
Ballad Singer (Actor's Name)	✔											
MacHeath (Actor's Name)	✔		✔	✔		✔	✔					✔
Jenny (Actress's Name)	✔					✔	✔		✔	✔		✔
Peachum ( )	✔	✔		✔				✔	✔			✔
Mrs Peachum ( )	✔	✔		✔		✔	✔	✔	✔			✔
Polly ( )	✔	✔	✔		✔			✔			✔	✔
Lucy ( )	✔							✔			✔	✔
Tiger Brown ( )	✔			✔				✔	✔			✔
Filch ( )	✔	✔										
Matt of the Mint ( )	✔		✔		✔							✔
Crook Fingered Jake ( )	✔		✔		✔		✔					✔

Knowing exactly when characters will appear helps you to plan your whole production.

REHEARSAL SPACE

With the settings designed you will know the physical dimensions of your production, and it is now important that you find a rehearsal space about the same size as the space in which the production will be performed. Spend pre-rehearsal time seeking a suitable venue. If the only space you can find is not ideal, work out ways of suiting it to your staging needs. Few rehearsal venues include a full stage setting area and you will have to decide well in advance what adjustments to make. Work out with your designer the best possible compromise. In some settings width is more important than depth, in others *vice versa*, so go for the best arrangement in terms of what you need.

If your production includes items like dances, fights or musical numbers you will need space to rehearse these too. Divide all of your rehearsals into 'big' and 'small', according to how many people will take part and what they will be doing, and allot the larger space to the bigger rehearsal even if you are not taking it.

OUTLINE REHEARSAL SCHEDULES

The rehearsal schedule is the backbone of a theatrical project. It does with time what the budget does with money, allowing you to measure and allocate it to the maximum benefit of players and production. Also, a group of voluntary, non-professional actors must know well in advance when and for how long they will be needed for rehearsal so that they may adjust the rest of their lives accordingly. Actors surprised by last-minute calls to rehearse, or worrying because they should be doing something else, cannot give you the performances you want. Respect their busy lives away from the theatre and they will work harder on the production.

Until you know who the actors are, an exact schedule is not possible, but your knowledge of the play and how you want to produce it will enable you to draft an outline schedule. You know how long you have until opening night so work back from that date to decide a first-rehearsal date that will let you develop the play in the detail you want. Be generous in allocating time. Superficial rehearsal is useless, and you cannot predict what problems of 'business' or interpretation may arise.

Work from the running time of each scene, allowing an initial rehearsal that gives you time to cover it properly. Do not underestimate the problems of short scenes; in the early days you should give *at least* half an hour to any scene.

Try to rotate scenes fairly regularly so that the cast do not forget the work they have done. Once you have an outline schedule you can discuss with the actors – as you cast them – what demands you will be making on their time.

Space, light and cleanliness are important in rehearsal rooms. Few of them are perfect, but do not settle for the squalid or unsafe.

The
Rehearsal
Room

WEEK ONE		TIME
1	FIRST REHEARSAL	7.00 - 10.00
2	BLOCK ACT I	7.00 - 10.00
3	BLOCK ACT I	7.00 - 10.00
WEEK TWO		
1	BLOCK ACT I	7.00 - 10.00
2	BLOCK ACT II	7.00 - 10.00
3	BLOCK ACT II	7.00 - 10.00
WEEK THREE		
1	BLOCK ACT II	7.00 - 10.00
2	WORK ACT I	7.00 - 10.00
3	WORK ACT I	7.00 - 10.00
4	WORK ACT II	2.00 - 6.00
WEEK FOUR		
1	WORK ACT II	7.00 - 10.00
2	WORK ACT I	7.00 - 10.00
3	WORK SCENES	7.00 - 10.00
4	WORK SCENES	3.00 - 10.00
WEEK FIVE		
1	RUN ACT I + NOTES	7.00 - 10.00
2	RUN ACT II + NOTES	7.00 - 10.00
3	RUN THROUGH PLAY + NOTES	7.00 - 10.00
4	RUN THROUGH PLAY + NOTES x 2	3.00 - 10.00
WEEK SIX		
M	TECHNICAL REHEARSALS	7.00 - 10.00
T	DRESS REHEARSAL	7.00 - 10.00
W	PERFORMANCE 1	7.30

PREPARING FOR CASTING

Having decided *how many* actors you will need, go through the play in detail and decide *what kind*. Before you audition anyone you must be quite clear about the specific requirements of each role in the production. If it entails music or singing, discuss this with the musical director, who will conduct the auditions with you. Simply getting actors to read or sing may not be enough. Devise things for them to do that will reveal their all-round suitability – or otherwise – for the roles.

A standardized approach to casting keeps your mind clear and is fair to the actors.

REHEARSAL ROOMS

The space to be used for rehearsals must be clean, properly ventilated, and well lit. It should be moderately comfortable, with clean toilets and an area where the actors can relax and take refreshments. You must have free access to the building, so avoid one without a caretaker regularly on duty or for which you cannot have sets of keys.

Safety is important. Do not accept inaccessible rehearsal rooms in run-down areas. This can have a bad effect on actors' attendance at rehearsals.

Character *Henry V*

Age to be played *27*

Physical type *Athletic* Height *5' 10"* Build

Type of character *Noble*

Special requirements

Vocal quality *N.A.*

Size of role *Leading*

Physical demands *Strenuous*

Fighting? *Sword.*

Dancing? *?*

Singing? *N.A.*

Comic ability required? *No.*

If musical rehearsal is part of the programme you will need a decent well-tuned piano. The rehearsal room will be your base until production week, so you will need an extra room for fitting costumes and wigs and space for scene-building and making properties. These cannot be done either efficiently or safely with actors in the rehearsal room.

REHEARSAL ROOM CHECKLIST

The points listed below are what a company should have to work at its best, but of course compromises may have to be made.

VENUE

Where is it?

Can it be reached by public transport?

Is there a telephone?

Is it available for the time we need it?

Is access easy?

Will we have keys?

Are the doors safe and well lit?

Are there any security problems?

How much space will we have?

Is it clean?

Is it properly ventilated?

Is it well lit?

Are there decent toilet facilities?

Are there refreshment facilities?

Is there additional space?

Is there a piano?

Are there keys to the piano?

CHAPTER 6

CASTING

Casting is when the director chooses the actors wanted to take part in a production. They should be auditioned for every role – and that includes actors whom the director knows. Type-casting and the casting of friends is risky. It is better to audition for a specific play than to determine generally how good an actor is, and any special skills required should also be tested at the audition. It is also wise to cast well in advance to accommodate drop-outs.

IS CASTING IMPORTANT?

As director you will spend more production time with the cast than with anyone else, so you must be able to work together in a friendly and relaxed way. Never cast actors whom you do not believe in or who clearly do not believe in you. You need an efficient and dedicated working group who respect each other's abilities. Social considerations are also important, and you may decide to take a willing but less talented actor rather than a brilliant one who will cause trouble or fail to mix with the others.

DECIDING WHAT YOU WANT

Casting is a heavy responsibility. Your decisions will affect a lot of people deeply, so try to be sensitive to their personalities as well as their talents. Be quite sure about what you want in any given character and seek the best actor for that role. Resist being pressured by anyone into casting someone whom you think is wrong for a part, but remember too that a good acting company is not just composed of excellent actors.

TYPECASTING

Typecasting has its pros and its cons. Typecast actors will respond quickly to your requests and give you something well within their range, but you may get no more than that, which can halt overall progress and development in rehearsals. The actor, too, may suffer from having the performance compared with a previous similar one.

CASTING FRIENDS

A director naturally wants to work with friendly and supportive colleagues, but the casting of friends needs careful thought. A rehearsal period can be a testing one for a friendship. Your friends will see you in a new, demanding *persona*, and may feel challenged, or simply threatened, by what you ask of them as actors, especially if you also want their support as friends.

Friendship with actors can blind you to their true abilities and lead you to giving them roles beyond or beneath them. The casting of friends may also be a disservice as it can mean exposing them to jealous comment. It is wiser to cast friends only if they are the best actors you know for the parts.

AUDITIONING

Only at an audition can you form an opinion about an actor's suitability for a role. Even one who has played the part before has not done so for you. You are looking for three things: the actor's general level of skill, the promise of specific skills and qualities needed for a role in a particular production, and the actor's willingness to work with you on the role. Your ultimate aim is a play with the strongest possible cast.

Even experienced actors get nervous at auditions. No one likes being graded and assessed. Try to put them at their ease by giving them *space* to prepare themselves and *enough time* to show you what they can really do. Ask auditionees to learn a short speech – twenty lines or so – appropriate to the play, and invite each one to audition at a definite time, thus avoiding a nerve-racked line of people at the door. Greet them personally and ask what they are interested in doing. Explain your approach to the production and ask each actor to perform the chosen speech. Reading auditions alone are rarely satisfactory, but ask the actor also to read a speech, giving time for preparation and some direction on mood, tempo or character. After the audition spend a minute chatting – without dashing or raising hopes, and without showing disappointment.

Avoid on-the-spot decisions and have a colleague present with whom to discuss the auditions – but not while actors are present. After these first auditions compile a shortlist of the actors who interested you for particular roles. If you are not sure about an actor invite him or her to audition again. You may want to see if certain actors are mutually compatible. Make detailed notes.

A useful audition needs planning, scheduling and budgeting. Be sure that your budget includes provision for it.

Explain the production to your actors. An us and them approach at auditions rarely produces good performances.

SPECIAL SKILL AUDITIONS

Singing, dancing or fighting should be tested at special auditions. Such sessions are best held with small groups rather than with individuals. Auditioning actors through improvisation should be done in the same way.

MAKING YOUR CHOICE

Choosing a cast from among the candidates can be difficult and painful. Using your notes, first eliminate all the actors you *do not* want, then work through the cast list, starting with the leading roles, and note possibilities among those you have not rejected. Discuss all this with your colleagues on the audition panel, then choose your cast. Though your decisions are final you should give weight to the others' opinions.

A hunch about an actor can be right, and an imperfect but exciting candidate may, by opening night, have a more interesting performance to offer than a competent all-rounder. Be ready to take some chances – while avoiding blatant risks.

REJECTIONS

When you have your full cast send out your rejection letters. Keep them short and do not give reasons for rejection. Being turned down is painful, and the actors may want to know why, so be polite but firm. Do not antagonize any of them. You may want them in future productions for which they are more suitable.

LETTING PEOPLE KNOW

Every actor who has auditioned should be told the outcome privately, preferably by letter, which avoids direct confrontation with disappointed candidates. Ask those you wish to cast to inform you promptly of their acceptance (or otherwise), and close with the date, time and venue of the first rehearsal. Write to successful candidates first. You may have to go back to your rejection list if someone turns down a part.

Type of audition	Space	Time	Extras
Character casting	Medium room + Waiting area	15 minutes per actor	Scripts of play Other texts
Singing	Medium room – low echo – + Warm-up room	15 minutes per actor	Piano Pianist Scores/music
Dance	Large room – sprung floor – + Rest area/Changing room	3 hours per group	Rosin trays Piano/music or good tape system
Acrobatic skills	Large room Mats + Rest room + Changing room	3 hours	Mats Equipment
Fighting	Large room – non-slip floor + Rest room	3 hours per group	Mats Weapons First aid
Improvisation	Medium room – smaller room – + Rest area	3 hours per group	Prop selection Chairs Tables Texts as required

CHAPTER 7

REHEARSALS

WHAT GOES ON IN REHEARSALS?

The play is broken into units and tested to find how the whole can be made to work at every performance. Spot things that could impair success and deal with them. Identify the units and suggest ways of looking at them. Pre-rehearsal work will show you:

- what happens in a scene
- who is in it and why
- why it is written as it is,

Share all this with the cast and get them to think about what the play demands of them. Their ideas may not be yours, and conflict can arise when you or they try a short cut or a too-elaborate route. The play itself is your target, and you must always keep that in sight.

Rehearsals should be hard work but not tense. If tension arises it is probably because the director is ill prepared or is prepared in only one way and cannot recognize the value of flexibility. Before a rehearsal starts establish what you want without being rigid about how to achieve it. If you do this the actors will be more convincing as they will be working on something they can understand.

As director you will be expected to have all the answers. Do not give them away all the time. If an actor is stuck try to discover why by retracing your steps to that point. Your solution to someone else's problem may not be the best one.

REHEARSAL SCHEDULES

Now is when you activate your rehearsal schedule. Each rehearsal has been planned to examine a particular part of the play, which you have defined through characters, their relationships and story elements, and should help *only* with the work you think necessary. Beware of separating actors who do not get on, or of working more with those who like you or work better with you.

LONG-TERM SCHEDULES

The 'master schedule' will plot all the production work you envisage and be your guideline, personal check-list and map right through from first rehearsal to second night. If you find yourself behind or ahead of the schedule find out why – quickly.

Remember, too, that all other departments work from the schedule, the production's backbone, and must be told at once of any major changes in it.

DAILY SCHEDULES

Each day's rehearsal is dictated by the master schedule, and here the flexibility needed in any complex operation can be expressed. You will know which actors are available and which part of the play is to be worked on. Decide your priorities within that space and organize accordingly.

For example, Day 22 of *She Stoops to Conquer* offers Act I Scene I with all actors available. It has already been well rehearsed but is not yet as you want it. The story is not clear, and the problem lies in the all-important Constance-Kate dialogue. We arrange Day 22's rehearsal to focus on this:

7.00 Kate and Constance
8.00 join Mr Hardcastle, Mrs Hardcastle
8.15 join Tony
8.45 run Act I Scene I and Notes
9.30 call ends

With 'daily' rehearsals make sure that:
■ you are rehearsing what needs it, not just repeating things
■ you plan far enough in advance to let actors know what they will be rehearsing and when
■ you do not go out of sequence unless you are confident about doing so.

BEFORE REHEARSAL BEGINS

Get to the rehearsal room early – on the first day with the stage manager, to mark up an outline of the set on the floor.

MARKING UP

Working from the designer's ground plan, mark out with coloured tape the lines the set's walls will take, indicating doors, windows, fireplaces and any changes in stage level. If the rehearsal room is smaller than your proper stage or setting give priority to that dimension of the set that is most important to staging. For example, if your main entrance is upstage make sure that the front of the stage is clearly marked, and go over this with the actors, explaining what it means and any differences between it and the actual set.

PROPS AND FURNITURE

Your preparatory work includes listing furniture and properties that the play requires. You will need good substitutes for them in rehearsals, so give the stage manager the lists well before the first session. Take these objects seriously and your actors will respect their importance in enhancing the world of the play. They also save a lot of time at dress rehearsals, helping to produce the polished result that you want.

Always clear the rehearsal stage after rehearsal. Time and effort will be saved if props can be locked away on the spot.

Though furniture will seldom be the same as that on stage, seek substitutes of roughly the same dimensions. This is especially important in comedy, where timing can be seriously affected by furniture dimensions.

WEEK	TECHNICAL + PRODUCTION NOTES	CAST NOT AVAILABLE	LOCATION	REHEARSAL
M	FINAL BUDGET MEET.		THEATRE CLUB	
T	DESIGN MEETING.		THEATRE CLUB	
F	PRODUCTION MEET.		THEATRE CLUB	
SU			YOUTH CLUB	1200 – 2000 : READ THROUGH + FIRST MEET.
T	COSTUME ⎫	MP / RR / SS	YOUTH CLUB	1900 – 2200 : ACT I
W	FITTINGS ⎬	MP	YOUTH CLUB	1900 – 2200 : ACT I
SU	BY ARR ⎭	MP	YOUTH CLUB	1500 – 2000 : ACT I
M	BUILDING SET⎤	BG / HR / RR	YOUTH CLUB	1900 – 2200 : ACT II
W		SS	YOUTH CLUB	1900 – 2200 : ACT II
T			YOUTH CLUB	1900 – 2200 : ACT II
SU	⎦		YOUTH CLUB	1500 – 2000 : ACT II
M	BUILDING SET⎤	RR	YOUTH CLUB	1900 – 2200 : ACT III
T		SS	YOUTH CLUB	1900 – 2200 : ACT III
W			YOUTH CLUB	1500 – 2200 : ACT III
SU	⎦		THEATRE CLUB	1500 – 2000 : ACT III
M	BUILDING ⎤ SET	RR	THEATRE CLUB	1900 – 2200 : ACT I
T	COSTUME ⎬	SS (UNTIL 2030)	THEATRE CLUB	1900 – 2200 : ACT I
W	FITTINGS ⎭		THEATRE CLUB	1900 – 2200 – ACT I
SU	⎦		THEATRE	1500 – 2000 : RUN ACT I
M	BUILDING SET⎤	RR	THEATRE	1900 – 2200 : ACT II
T			THEATRE	1900 – 2200 : ACT II
W			THEATRE	1900 – 2200 : RUN ACT II
SU	PAINTING ⎦		THEATRE (TO 1800) THEN R/ROOM.	1500 – 2000 : ACT III
M	PAINTING	RR	CLUB R/ROOM	1900 – 2200 : ACT III
T			CLUB R/ROOM	1900 – 2200 : RUN ACT III
W			CLUB R/ROOM	1900 – 2200 : ACT I + NOTES
TH			CLUB R/ROOM	1900 – 2200 : ACT I + NOTES
S			CLUB R/ROOM	1500 – 2000 : ACT II + III NOTES
T	1800 – 2200 ⎤		R/ROOM	1900 – 2200 : NOTES (ACT III)
W	1800 – 2200 ⎬ SETTING BUILDING		R/ROOM	1900 – 2200 : RUN THROUGH
TH	1800 – 2200 ⎭		R/ROOM	1900 – 2200 : RUN THROUGH
SA	1000 – 1700 TECH + LIGHTS		THEATRE	1400 – 1700 : LIGHT + TECH
SU	1000 – 1700 TECH WORK		THEATRE	1900 : DRESS REHEARSAL ①
M			THEATRE	1730 : DRESS REHEARSAL
T			THEATRE	17.30 : PERFORMANCE ①
W			THEATRE	1730 : PERFORMANCE ②
TH			THEATRE	1730 : PERFORMANCE ③
F			THEATRE	1730 : PERFORMANCE ④
S			THEATRE	1730 : PERFORMANCE ⑤
SU	STRIKE SET		THEATRE	
M	RETURNS.			

THE FIRST REHEARSAL

Everyone – including you – will be nervous, but you must try not to show it. As director you are in a strong position. The others are there because you believe you can all work together. If you are well prepared you have no reason to worry.

HOW TO TACKLE IT

The audience will see a whole play, but you and the cast will be seeing it bit by bit, putting it together over the coming weeks. Do not put on an impressive 'director' act. You are with colleagues who want to know what you think, but who are equals. You have to work *together*.

You are half way through your work; the actors are just starting. Do not flash your knowledge and preparation around; share it. Tell your cast the problems – and the objective, putting on a good show by solving them. Above all make it clear that you think your cast can solve *any* problems.

DIRECTOR'S INTRODUCTION

Most actors read a play with their own roles mainly in mind. You read it for its total effect. In your introduction state clearly:

■ what you think the play's story is (try to get this down to three simple sentences)
■ how you think the author tells that story
■ how you propose telling it from the stage.

What the play *means* is not so important at this stage; right now what is needed is a simple, clear objective, challenging but not impossible, that excites the actors without intimidating them.

GETTING A RELAXED CAST

The director must retain power without intimidating anyone. Avoid 'schoolroom' situations. Greet each actor on arrival, introduce yourself and others to anyone you don't know and aim to achieve an informal and enjoyable atmosphere. Do not spend time with old friends at the expense of strangers. Tea and coffee at the first session

encourage group relaxation. After a reasonable time, with everyone present and a circle of chairs having been set out, ask them to join you rather than ordering a start.

GETTING STARTED: YOU HAVE SEVERAL CHOICES

Now comes the crunch. Everyone has met and you have had your say. What next? This depends on several things, but your choices after a talk are:

■ working session
■ read-through
■ 'blocking' of the play
■ read-through and discussion.

Remember that your cast may not have done much work yet, so you are likely to dominate discussion at the first rehearsal. If discussion is to be your starting point:

■ state this when you hand out scripts, and ask people to read the play in advance
■ be prepared to hear others' viewpoints
■ be prepared to talk a lot.

Some directors like to start on page one and start arranging the moves (blocking). Most actors like this as it is *doing* rather than thinking or talking. Be sure that you think this is right for the play and be prepared to do the major part yourself, planning exits, entrances and major moves.

The talk-read-through is especially useful on period plays, whose language may be unfamiliar, but to be successful it needs time. Be prepared for actors who consider this approach 'academic', boring and irritating. Even if the play is a serious one keep the discussion light and avoid dominating it unless it flags. Above all make clear your own interpretation of the play.

However, actors basically *do* – that is they act – and so all discussion should lead to practical expression.

Early rehearsals need a flexible approach. Let the actors experiment but be ready with instructions when necessary.

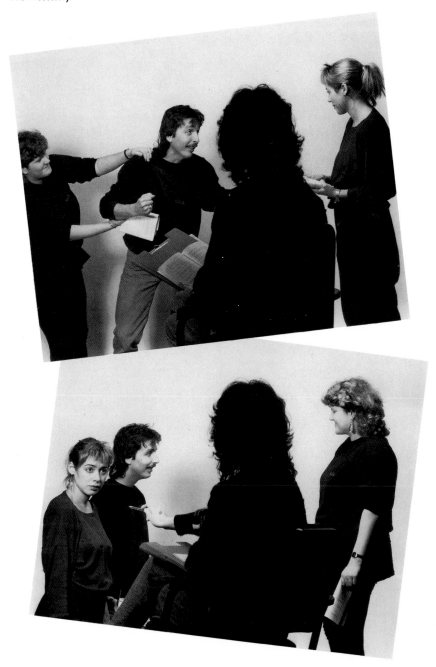

FURTHER REHEARSALS

You will be at all rehearsals, and you may feel that the play has taken over your life. Counter this and keep the others alert by varying approaches to the work. Though continuity is essential, avoid a rut.

AVOIDING ROUTINE

Must you rehearse the play in its sequence? Once you are clear on the storyline try breaking it into units. Rehearse those scenes involving particular characters or having one theme. This will help you and the cast to see how an idea is developed; will allow work in depth; and will vary scheduling.

Games and exercises can be useful here. Place them at different points in the session for maximum effect.

CALLING THE CAST

In your daily rehearsal schedule be economical with actors' time. People kept waiting can lose interest. Especially towards the end of the rehearsal period actors will appreciate your consideration. Much better to call fewer actors for a long rehearsal than to call many and not use them.

REHEARSAL TARGETS

Set yourself rehearsal targets – at first broad ones like examining a particular scene or character, but later more specific ones. Look at each scene and decide what you think is not working. Focus on that in rehearsal and correct it. But do not 'press on regardless'. You may have set up something that your cast cannot play.

REHEARSAL CALL

SHOW   THE THREEPENNY OPERA

DATE   *9th Sept '88*

PLACE   *The Vanburgh Theatre*

10.30 AM	ACT 2 SC. 5	MISS TUCKER MRS EVANS
12.00	ACT 2 SC. 4	MISS GARDEN MR EVANS
1.00 PM	LUNCH BREAK	
2.00 PM	ACT 1 SC 2	MISS GARDEN MR CERQUIRA MR DUFF MR EVANS MR HAREWOOD
3.00 PM	ACT 1 SC	MR MCKINVEW TO JOIN
4.00 PM	SOLOMON SONGS	MISS TUCKER
4.30 PM	ACT 3 SC 8	MISS GARDEN MISS MCDONNELL
5.30 PM	BREAK	
6.30 PM	RUN OF ACT 2 FOLLOWED BY NOTES	FULL COMPANY
8.00 PM	CALL ENDS	

SIGNED BY D.S.M.

The second stage is rehearsal in detail. Avoid calling actors who will not be needed.

Blocking takes time. Keep the rehearsal interesting but relaxed while explaining what you want.

BLOCKING THE PLAY

Much subsequent rehearsal will be spent on 'blocking' the play, when actors' movements are examined and decided upon. You may do this as part of examining the text and spend a rehearsal elucidating the physical expression of the play's meaning. Or you may work out the main movements in advance and spend time getting the actors to do them. The latter, time-honoured method is worth considering, especially with inexperienced casts in music theatre and in crowded scenes. Always remember the 'why' of each move and explain it to the actor when 'blocking'.

MOVEMENT

What we see on stage is as important as what we hear. We respond to images before words, so you must guide your cast to express *physically* the characters they play. While understanding their parts, inexperienced actors may have movement problems that hamper expression because of how they move in real life. They think like the characters but move as themselves.

Actors' whole bodies must take part in their roles, so watch how your actors use theirs. Often you will find that only a part of the body has been recruited to the role. Warm-ups at the start of sessions relax the actors and prepare them for that conscious use of their bodies on stage that they restrain in everyday life.

TRUST

You are asking people to behave, act and even think extraordinarily, so some self-consciousness is inevitable. Your cast, asked to put themselves in your hands, have to feel that what you want is essential to the play. Be sure that however well a move suits a character the actor understands it and is happy with it. You must reciprocate your actors' trust that you will not make them look foolish. If you are not honest with actors about how they appear, someone else may be, and that can be destructive. If your notes are clearly honest, considerate and constructive, the actors will accept them. 'Superior' or sarcastic notes will make a cast feel inadequate and/or resentful.

IMAGINING AND PICTURING

You may have visual ideas, but only words to communicate them. Heighten your message to an actor with simple visual images. For example describe his or her speech as a lassoo and the other actor as a gatepost, meaning that the speaker must surround the listener with the speech, not let it fall short.

Encourage actors to think visually, especially in static or 'wordy' plays (see Chapter 8 for games and exercises in imagination and physicalization).

Telling detail can be added even to quite straightforward plays by getting actors to be very specific about material aspects of the characters they play. They should have a clear idea of the age, physical build, social background, enthusiasms and preferences in food, drink and clothing of their characters – even of their views on subjects that the play does not touch on. Examining and deciding about these matters gives the company a common topic – and it can be fun.

Work to build up trust from your cast rather than just demanding it.

ACTION

What a character *does* is sometimes hard to deduce from the text but you must make actors understand what they are doing throughout the play. Otherwise they cannot tell their parts of the story. Ask an actor to explain the character's actions (using the third person separates actor and role), then compare the account with what the actor does. You will both detect things like unnecessary detail, or crucial actions being unclear or omitted.

PLAYING

A problem in performing can be that actors' actions do not put across their understanding of the roles. Some ideas simply do not 'play' because actor and director are attempting the impossible: doing too many things at once or trying to act something that is not an action. Look at the text with the actor and decide what the character *does*. Then decide *how*. Can your 'how' be expressed in action? Often it cannot, but you know *what* the character does and that can be played. Do not indulge the audience with comment on what is played unless the work's style needs it.

Use directions to bridge what the author saw and what an actor does.

AUTHOR'S STAGE DIRECTION :

NURSE : I have given all and lost all in her service. Oh gods I have been paid my price.

                    EXIT

KEYNOTES OF THE ACTOR'S PERFORMANCE

Character: OLD
Mood: DESPAIRING
Next Action: SUICIDE
Attitude: RESIGNATION
Quality: DIGNITY

DIRECTOR INSTRUCTS

Your last moment with the audience. Remind them of who you have been. Get them to <u>think</u> about you.

ACTOR PLAYS

Sudden realisation- Moment of calm- <u>Tell</u> the audience - Leave slowly indicating pain and endurance.

ATTITUDES

Many actors unconsciously reveal their own attitudes to the characters. Watch for those inviting an audience to laugh at them in comedy or who play for sympathy in serious plays. The solution is, again, to clarify the action of the sequence with the actor. Then, if he or she plays it properly, there will be little time for anything else and the performance will be cleaner.

As director you will have specific ideas and must be clear about them to the cast. But be selective, and do not show off. If frustration makes you want to play a role that an actor is not doing right indulge yourself a little – if only to let off steam – but on opening night *you* will not be on stage; you must get the *actor* to make it work. Avoid doing everything for the actors and having them imitate you. It is bad for them – and for the play.

Is the director really helping the actor here?

WATCHING AND LISTENING

Sometimes you will feel you are expected to do everything, but two things you *must* do: watch and listen to your actors. You may be no actor yourself, but by observing what they do and how they say things you will learn more about acting than from any text book. You should develop this faculty, along with the ability to report accurately and objectively what you observe.

REMEMBERING

An anxiety-provoking feature of rehearsal is when something works wonderfully once, then never again. To counter this you must prime the cast every time a scene is repeated, and for that you need to develop a 'production memory'. Your stage manager should keep an up-to-date copy of all moves in the production, but you must remember how they were arrived at, why they were chosen and how the actors got that particular effect. Share with them your understanding of their work and analyse how things go right as well as wrong.

THE DIRECTOR AND THE STAGE

Your performance space can be an ally or an enemy. You must know its strengths and weaknesses and work with them throughout production. If your conception of the play is to be realized you must keep in mind the qualities of the stage while planning sets, blocking and rehearsing in depth. Otherwise you will be depressed by the difference between what you imagined and what you see, and will have to work overtime adjusting the production.

FOCUS

A good production is one that *the whole audience can see all the time*. That said, use the stage to focus their attention on what you feel are the play's important areas, not just by textual emphasis but also by positioning actors for visual emphasis. Any position on stage uses the stage's width and depth. How the audience perceives this use depends on the particular stage, which must be kept in mind when you block the play.

WIDTH AND DEPTH

Something you will be correcting throughout rehearsals is the moment when two actors find themselves standing in a line parallel to the audience. This gives the audience too much to think about; the actors demand equal attention, so which one is to be watched? If both actors must be on stage remember that:

■ they are 'read' better when they are farther apart
■ the one nearer the centre will have more 'importance'
■ stage depth must be considered, as, other things being equal, actor's 'importance' decreases with distance from the audience.

USING STAGE DEPTH

The 'other things being equal' above is the key to using depth. The actor nearer the audience is not *necessarily* more important. Positioned in profile or looking away from the audience, he or she has less 'weight' than a more distant one facing the audience.

The positions between on-stage actors and their audience may be seen as a series of triangles. When blocking the play imagine lines connecting them. If the lines become curves your staging will be weakened, so aim for the straightest, most direct ones. This helps actors to communicate efficiently, as well as allowing the audience a clear view of the actors and their interactions.

🔲 *VISIBILITY & IMPORTANCE DIMINISH UPSTAGE* 🔲 *DISTANCE BETWEEN ACTORS AIDS VISIBILITY*

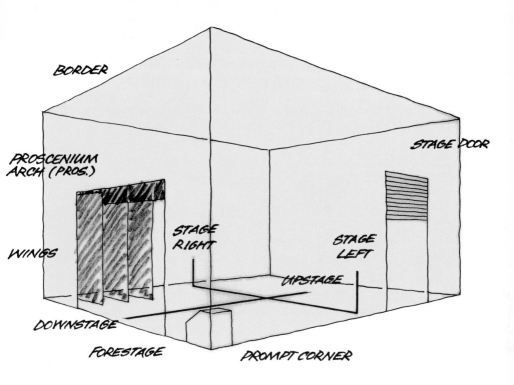

BORDER

PROSCENIUM ARCH (PROS.)

STAGE DOOR

STAGE RIGHT

STAGE LEFT

WINGS

UPSTAGE

DOWNSTAGE

FORESTAGE

PROMPT CORNER

THE PROSCENIUM STAGE

Once the commonest type of playing space, the proscenium arch stage is rarer now that big assembly areas must serve more functions than those of occasional theatre. Still, a director will often have to use a proscenium stage, and it is highly suitable for many kinds of theatre.

The proscenium presents the play to the audience in a 'picture-frame', with curtains that can cut them off from it when the story demands. Illusion is important in proscenium theatre, and many plays written for it are done so under a convention that largely assumes actors and audience not to be in the same space, the play being watched through a 'fourth wall'.

This type of stage has provided a standard terminology for positioning and moving actors, being divided into a nine-part grid, each part named by its position in relation to the audience. The strongest position is that of

Centre Stage. Upstage Centre and Centre are less 'powerful' than Downstage Centre. The Upstage areas are weaker still when furniture is on stage and should be used carefully. Upstage Centre is useful for important entrances, but no one should linger there – unless acting reluctance to enter.

Any part of the proscenium stage can be made the focal one. Just which part is dictated by technical needs connected with important 'business', for example', a scene with the burning of a letter in a fireplace. The letter must be visible to the whole house, but not at centre stage as that is too obstructive; also the fireplace must be sited plausibly. Whenever the focal area is other than Down Centre be sure to adjust the set so that the relation between the 'room' and the characters in it seems natural and spontaneous. That done, do not oppose it with right angles and straight lines, which look stiff and uncomfortable, destroying illusion.

THE THRUST STAGE

This is more than it may seem at first sight – just an extension of the proscenium stage. Its forward area is more important than the one behind the proscenium, suggesting spaces or 'rooms' that can no longer contain the emotions and energies of the characters, who themselves can no longer be contained within the illusory 'stage room' and need a greater reality through more direct relations with the audience. Classical plays, especially seventeenth- and eighteenth-century ones, and the so-called 'epic' theatre, all of which show high awareness of the audience, thrive in this staging.

The upstage centre area is again the strongest entrance place, gaining further strength from being seen in a wider perspective. Upstage left and upstage right are relatively weak on the thrust stage but useful for characters who are hiding, plotting or spying on downstage ones.

As its name implies, the thrust stage tends to throw the action forward. Guard against over-using its downstage centre emphasis.

Experiment with the added depth that the thrust stage provides by placing actors at greater distances apart, using one as a 'camera' focusing on the other. When 'double focus' demands that you show the feelings of both speaker and listener the upstage actor can play to the downstage one's back with great effect.

As with the proscenium stage, try to avoid parallel line groupings, which on the thrust stage diminish the statures of both actors rather than equalizing them.

THEATRE-IN-THE-ROUND

Mainly a reaction against the director's status as controller of who and what will be seen and when, theatre-in-the-round has its actors surrounded by an audience who, in theory, can look at any part of the stage that interests them. Any play can be performed 'in the round', but the method makes illusions hard to sustain for the whole audience and has problems with the height and positioning of furniture.

As some of the audience will be above the actors' heads the floor pattern of their movements is important. The audience must be able to tell from such an actor's move:

■ why it takes place
■ how energetic it is
■ what developments in the character it indicates.

Theatre-in-the-round thrives with a real ensemble but is disastrous unless the actors have total control of their performances. Each one must be a self-focusing automatic camera, always switched on but operating only at certain required moments – not always when the actor is speaking.

Paradoxically theatre-in-the-round has visibility problems. The 'equal' acting space can quickly be monopolized. *Distance* your actors from each other to distinguish them and give clarity to their performances. *Straight lines* and *sharp focus* are a necessity here – as they are in any staging. The analogy of theatre-in-the-round with the boxing ring should be your reminder that actors need *not* fight each other to be noticed.

When you are rehearsing for this type of stage *rehearse in the round*, and move about regularly so that you see the play's shape from every angle.

THE BLACK BOX

The black box studio is a common feature of educational and community centres. As its name implies the performing space is rectangular and painted dark to enable sharp focusing of light. Audience seating is flexible and technical installations similar to theatre in the round.

Like theatre in the round the black box allows any preferred arrangement between actors and audience. Its advantages are:

■ it lets you turn any safe room with minimum staging requirements into a theatre
■ it is totally flexible and adaptable to your needs
■ it conduces to great intimacy, benefiting young actors who lack conventional 'techniques'
■ it is the most easily simulated stage when rehearsing; if something works then it is likely to go almost as well in the black box theatre.

Here again the emphasis is on creating strong, clear relations between the characters that the audience can see. Despite its simplicity the black box can provide powerful and exciting theatre. Never waste it by cluttering it with furniture and props. Clear direct storytelling is its strength, so the actors must be well versed in the play's action, characters, their movements and their positions. The black box ruthlessly reveals any lack of preparation or understanding. Avoid this and you can put on memorable theatre.

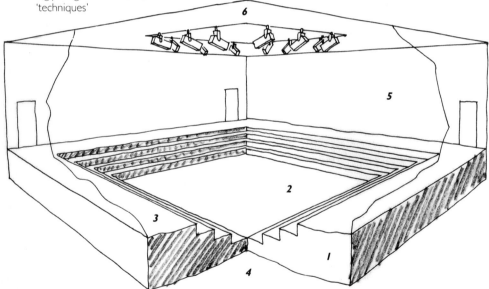

BLACK BOX NOTES

1 Tiered seating improves the whole audience's visibility.
2 A rectangular acting area is less flexible, less dynamic, than in the round or thrust.
3 Secondary acting areas, available behind seating tiers, are always invisible to some of the audience.
4 The four main entrances at the corners of the acting area.
5 Black walls are confining and create a claustrophobic atmosphere
6 The lighting rig is usually invisible. (Note that the black box can be stripped to basic seating and equipment for more flexibility.)

OPEN-AIR STAGING

The natural setting that inspires so many open-air productions can be your worst enemy (after the weather!). To keep the setting in the audience's eye you may have to choose a stage area that brings problems with it. Open-air stages are bigger-scale than indoor ones and you may find that your actors are being dwarfed by real trees and buildings.

Look for a space with a background that does not stretch to the horizon. Trees make an excellent 'back wall', with interesting daylight vistas and scope for dramatic lighting.

Seating is in standard units unless you build your own. Avoid the 'grandstand' effect and place your seating to create strong focal points on stage. Here the thrust stage and theatre in the round should be your models rather than the proscenium.

Because of open-air theatre's big scale, entrances and exits must be prepared carefully and the time they will take allowed for. They should also be in character.

Open-air theatre can be exciting, but be sure *you are staging the play*, not just using the setting.

ACTING AND THE DIRECTOR

Pinpointing the action The most important thing in a play is *what happens*. It is what the audience sees and what the actors must know before there can be a performance. Your actors have to be clear about it, so you must be.

Read the play, see how the whole action is presented and decide what each character contributes. Discuss with the actors what happens and listen carefully to their comments. In rehearsal, questions like 'What happens here?' and 'What do you want?' can be hard to answer. An actor may offer a complicated answer. Instead of rejecting it, work it through and help the actor to understand *what the character* knows about the story at any given point. Actors may base characterizations on their knowledge of the whole play, which endangers the unfolding story. Plays often show people changing in the face of unusual circumstances; the differences between them at the beginning and at the end must be preserved. In acting the *changes* are important.

MOTIVATION

Every action on stage must be motivated by a need or desire that the character is understood to have. A move aimed simply at getting an actor into a better position is *dramatically* impossible. There must be a plausible *why* (in terms of the character) for the action, and you must know *why* before you can say *how*.

Motivation can be determined by answering the simple question: 'What does the character want?' The answer – 'X wants Y' or 'X wants to do Z' – should be simple and may even be banal. Never mind. The desire itself may be banal. Simplicity of meaning is one of the theatre's strengths.

You may find that at a certain point a character wants something else. Think of such individual wants as bricks to be shaped and proportioned into a wall. Never mind inconsistencies. Few plays would be written if characters had to be consistent – but they must be plausible in the playwright's terms.

EXITS AND ENTRANCES

Work on these tends to be left until last at rehearsals, with the excuse 'it depends on what goes before' or 'we've no proper doors yet', so in many productions characters sidle on and slink off – good acting trying to cope with poor preparation.

Characters' entrances and exits are as important to the play as the scenes themselves and must be played accordingly. Actors must understand *and convey* why they enter and/or leave a room. To enter is to bring motivated energy on stage. To exit is to remove it. Your cast must know why they come on and what they want when they come on and must take up positions likely to help them get it. They should be working towards these from the moment they appear. Similarly beware a scene being 'left' on stage when the actor exits. Departure too must be motivated; the actor must know *and act* the reason for leaving. The character must *stay alive* until the actor is out of sight. Even as a timid or tentative character the actor must be confident about the why and how of entrances and of exits.

MAKING AN ENTRANCE

Before making an entrance the actor must decide:—

1. The age and status of character.
2. What the character has just done before entering.
3. By what means the character reached the point of entry. (Stairs? Driveway? etc.).
4. The character's mood *before* entering.
5. The character's *reason* for coming into the room or place of action.
6. The means of entering (door, window, gate, floor, sky).

MAKING AN EXIT

The character must remain alive until the exit is completed. To ensure this work out :—

1. What has happened to the character in the scene preceding.
2. *How* the character appears different to the audience now at the end of the scene.
3. The character's mood (happy, sad,).
4. Does the character *decide* to leave or is it *told* to go?
5. Has the character won or achieved anything?
6. Has the character lost anything?
7. The path by which the actor will leave the stage. It *must* be clear to be strong.

Always rehearse the positions, pace and timing of exits and entrances.

PROBLEMS ON STAGE

Strong and weak positions

A strong position is one in which an actor is seen and heard by the audience while playing vital actions. In such a position the actor can control the surrounding area and be the focal centre on stage and for the audience. A weak position is one that prevents an actor achieving the effects in action and character required by the play at that point.

In such a case you should look at two things:

The actor's position:
■ is anyone upstage of the 'focused' actor?
■ if so what is the upstage actor doing?
■ does the 'focused' actor need to contact the upstage one?

The actor's body angle:
■ can the audience see the 'focused' actor?
■ can the other actors see the 'focused' actor?
■ is the 'focused' actor's position dictated by having to contact others in stronger positions?

In all these cases the supposedly 'focused' actor isn't focused!

A weak position is simply one that does not let the actor move the story along as required. When it happens, go over each step of the scene to find out *how*, then *rework the scene*. Changing position on the spot is merely cosmetic, covering cracks that could later bring down the whole structure, as well as using movement to get out of staging problems instead of to tell the story.

MOVEMENT

Movement is the actor's main means of expression. The body can eloquently reinforce spoken words – or belie them – so an actor's every on-stage movement must express understanding of the character's feeling about the words.

Untrained actors are less skilled with their bodies than with words so they need their director's help. The problem will be two-fold: physical (the body cannot do it) or interpretive (the body does not know how). Remember, too, that you cannot get every effect from everyone. In fast expansive moves and gestures a short-limbed actor will look different from a long-limbed one. Never ask actors to express things that are beyond them or make them look foolish.

Physical problems are often connected with tension or not using the whole body. The next chapter deals extensively with actors' body problems.

Interpretive problems arise when an actor knows what is wanted but is not expressing it. You should ask yourself the three following questions:

■ has the actor prepared the movement?

The body must be programmed to express and underline rapid changes of mind in the character. Every movement has a beginning, a middle and an end which may be thought of as relax-tense-relax, and the actor must know these even if only the middle is shown. Movements made under tension do not read. They are noticed but may not be properly understood.

■ has the actor focused the movement?

Each movement must have an object – a thing or person – and that object must be clear to the audience. Do not cheat here. The actor may not be centred on the movement's recipient. Thinking 'out front' rather than to the character's focus makes the straight line a curve, weakening the movement. Tension goes and the action becomes indirect.

■ Does the speed of the movement help expression?

Moves must be 'read' by an audience, and doing them at real-life speed may be unhelpful. Try to judge the speed in terms of:

■ how well it expresses the character's feeling at that point
■ how much information it conveys (too much is as bad as too little)
■ how 'clean' it is (the move may be messy because the whole body is not in one focus)
■ whether words or gestures are blocking the effect the actor wants to convey.

ESTABLISHING FOCUS

You may differ with an actor about the focus of an action. Discuss and establish:

■ whom the mover is addressing or approaching
■ where that person or object is on the stage
■ how important the move is.

An actor's movement towards another actor or object closes the distance between them, making the mover visible to less of the audience, closing the focus and perhaps diminishing the mover's importance.

Always ask *why* and *how* a move is made, *how* it helps to tell the story and *where* it leaves the mover when complete. Instead of moving, a character might stay still but be made more important by being turned to by others.

Focus: the actor focuses the attention on what and who motivates the rise.

Preparation: know why your character moves and ensure that all physical work is prepared. This actor must focus on what makes the rise — prepare the hands to free the body, and establish the direction.

Speed: the actor responds precisely to what causes the rise. The speed reflects the mood, urgency, and intention.

THE ACTOR AND THE TEXT

What does it mean? In many plays the meaning is clear, but in some complex ones it is rather less so. A play written in another time, in an unfamiliar style or in translation from a foreign language will raise basic questions of meaning for the director and actors. You must know the play's background and, if possible, why it was written; you must explain simply what you think the author means at any point. Be ready to do a lot of homework and encourage the actors to do the same. Every line and action in the play must have an understood meaning, even if you want to make more complex statements about them. Complex ideas seldom 'play' well, and in performance will show up confusions of meaning or understanding.

LINES AND CUES

Actors tend to think in terms of lines and cues, and these are a part of learning the play. But your cast must grow beyond that stage to thinking of the piece as a series of feelings, thoughts and conversations. The words are merely a starting point for the rich interplay of impressions, understandings and stimuli comprised by good theatre, whatever the play. Best results will be obtained if the cast master lines and cues early, then in rehearsal learn to listen and feel.

Announce a time beyond which you will not work with actors still reading their lines – and stick to it. It is in every-one's best interest.

Reading from a script holds up the acting. Get your actors to work from memory as soon as possible to avoid confusion.

PROMPTING

The prompter's function is to remind actors of forgotten lines or to supply missed cues. The voice of the prompter is always disruptive and destroys any illusion created. Actors should therefore be encouraged to improvise their way out of trouble.

If a prompter is unavoidable make sure that they are placed where they can see the actors *and* the script. A good prompter needs a clear carrying voice, must be alert, sufficiently familiar with the production to know actor's pauses, and must not be nervous about being audible. It is not a job for an inexperienced actor or a shy stage manager. Make sure that the actors and prompter establish a clear procedure for the taking of prompts. The best thing for the actor is simply to say 'line please.'

THOUGHT

The actor on stage must communicate the character's thought processes. This is a most exciting quality of good acting. It is achieved, like so much in acting, by the actor being so in control of the role that listening and watching become the character's main activities. Thought cannot be faked.

SPONTANEITY AND CREATIVITY

You will have the most information and knowledge about the play, but do not let that stifle spontaneity or creativity. Present information as material to be explored creatively through acting. What matters in the end is what the audience sees and hears, not what you and your cast know.

PROBLEM	EXPLANATION	COURSE OF ACTION
The actor has become monotonous	Tiredness	Break or move on to something fresh
	Lack of information	Go through the speech again
	Feels trapped	Encourage movement
The actor is overplaying	Wants to show off	Ask about character and context
	Actor is compensating for uncertainty	Take the pressure off. Go slowly and sit down.
Action is static	The actor has not combined action and character	Let actor move the scene. Play games. Isolate action from character.
Actor in wrong position	Forgotten right one	Remind from S.M. copy.
	Doesn't agree it's right	Discuss.
Actor fidgeting	Wants to move	Encourage movement.

WINDING UP

Assessment and direction

As director you had an aim at the start of the session. Did you achieve it? What else must be done to achieve it? What else was achieved? What next?

These questions will be in the cast's mind so you must face them. Don't say things are OK if they are not – and don't resent the best idea or most successful solution coming from someone else.

WHAT DID I WANT?	DID I GET IT?	<u>YES</u> → WHAT DO I WANT NEXT ? <u>NO</u> → WHY NOT ? → HOW CAN I BE MORE CLEAR? → DO I WANT THE RIGHT THING?

Being honest

Rehearsals are the tip of the iceberg. Actors do a lot of unseen work beforehand and you should recognize it publicly. Similarly if little seems to be getting done mention it. It is best to take an erring actor aside for a private word in case there are extenuating circumstances.

If the discontent seems general, a brief pointed rebuke is in order – but not too often. Be sure that your contribution is not a prime cause of the apathy.

Administrative

Always tell your actors what they will be rehearsing next time and when it will be, preferably at the end of the session to avoid interrupting work.

Saying thanks

Finally, remember to say thank you, a small enough thing but conducive to a good atmosphere next time.

AFTER THE REHEARSAL

WITH ACTORS
- *Give notes <u>always</u>*
- *Tell actors <u>when</u> their next rehearsal is and <u>where</u>.*

WITH STAGE MANAGER Discuss
- *Any text changes*
- *Changes in blocking*
- *Added or deleted props*
- *Special costume notes*
- *Design considerations*
- *Anything needed for next rehearsal*

WITH DESIGNER Discuss
- *Props additions or deletions*
- *Specific action requirements*
- *Costume*
- *Light*
- *How the show is shaping up*

WITH THE PRODUCTION TEAM
- *Discuss any changes*
- *Look at work being completed*
- *Take an interest in their work.*

DIRECTOR
PREPARE FOR NEXT REHEARSAL.

Does an actor want your notes just now? Choose
the moment if you want it to work.
Make your notes succinct and positive. The show
must go somewhere from here. Respect the
cast's work for you and be honest about problems
with those who can take it.

CHAPTER 8

GAMES AND EXERCISES

Games and exercises can be useful in rehearsals, relaxing actors and building confidence and trust between them. They must be closely supervised and all safety measures taken beforehand.

Exercises are more specifically related to performing and interpreting skills and techniques than games, but playing games is an activity essential to theatre, for however convinced an audience may be, what it sees is not real. Game-playing is the first skill we develop, our first means of relating and responding to others. The most complex acting situation can be reduced to simple games that help an actor to see the point of a scene.

HOW TO USE GAMES

Basically games have three uses:

■ to relax the actors – invaluable for those coming from other daytime activities
■ to take the pressure off actors having production or interpretation problems and show through analogy how a difficult or 'wordy' scene should be played
■ as games are mainly physical, actors often respond to them better than to detailed verbal instructions.

GAMES FOR RELAXATION

These can be embodied in a brief warm-up. Some directors avoid warm-ups, feeling more secure behind the text, but they help actors to work together and concentrate on the rehearsal. Growing physical proficiency makes actors realize how they regress when rehearsing with books in their hands, and weans them from the book on to real acting.

WARM-UPS

The cast take off shoes and cumbersome clothing and stand in a circle, far enough apart to raise and circle their arms without touching each other, then follow the outline exercises below. Repeat each one about ten times at first, extending this as flexibility grows. Do not push too hard, and watch out for anyone having difficulty. *Always do the exercises with your actors.*

Head rolls

Place the feet about 30cm (12 in) apart and relax the shoulders. Drop the head forward on to the chest and roll it slowly clockwise over the right shoulder until it is upright. Let it fall back on chest and roll it anticlockwise to the left shoulder, then down.

Shoulder lifts

Standing as above, hands at sides and head upright but relaxed, lift both shoulders to a slow count of three, then drop them. Vary the speed with each repetition.

Arms

Standing as above, raise the extended right arm to shoulder height to a count of ten, then lower it. Repeat with the left arm. Vary speeds with repetitions.

Back

With feet apart and arms hanging free, drop the torso fully forward without straining, then return slowly to upright. *Important*: the back is delicate, and this exercise should be taken very slowly until actors are relaxed enough to flop from the hips and touch their toes.

Legs

The cast lie on the floor and relax (check that they *are* relaxed; tense positions are easily spotted), raise one leg at a time, move it back and forth from the knee, then describe circles in the air with it. Repeat with the other leg. When this is complete the actors rise *slowly* and play some games.

Rag dolls and tin soldiers

With the cast again standing in a circle ask them to be by turns rag dolls (floppy, slumped forward, totally relaxed) and tin soldiers (upright, taut, on parade). Request these alternately, then randomly. The results are relaxing and can be hilarious.

Watch your group for particular performing problems and try to invent games and exercises to solve them.

Join in games. Let your actors enjoy each other's work and keep the session moving.

Machines

Group the actors in threes or fives (not even numbers), then ask each group to be a machine (unnamed) and each of its members a machine part, contributing to a product. The groups perform in turn, the others guessing at the products and commenting on efficiency. Keep this part of the session short and lively.

Charades

In this old-fashioned parlour game every action can tell a story. It encourages physical economy, use of the body and freedom of performing. Pick a category – films, novels, great paintings and so on – and ask each actor to express one while the others guess what it is.

Ball games

These are useful in building concentration and mutual dependence. The simple ones are best.

'Going mad'

Actors are most inhibited when performing emotional extremes. Allow a little explosion at every rehearsal in which they may run wild, scream, shout and laugh. But keep it brief and be sure it is safe.

TAKING THE PRESSURE OFF

Rehearsals can easily be fraught. An actor may not be giving what you want, the ideas may be hard to play or you may not be giving a clear instruction – all of which can cause rising tempers and depression. Divert your cast from such a crisis with games.

Your most powerful tool is that *this is only a play*; it will not work unless approached with the freedom and confidence of children playing. Do not *say* this – your actors will feel patronized – but show it through mainly physical games that return them to what they can do and enjoy.

FOCUSING THROUGH GAMES

Actors can get tired and bored in a long scene that loses its edge and becomes difficult simply by taking so much time and thought. Refocus your cast's attention by having them play such simple, energetic games as tag, jumping up and down, 'going mad' and so on.

HELPING INTERPRETATION

The commonest interpretative problems arise out of failure to understand, to listen or to communicate. Games can help actors usefully in these areas:

Understanding

'Talk the actors through' the problem passage quickly and clearly, then get them to act it out in their own words. This will show where the problem is and what work has to be done. If actors mock a scene they find difficult watch how they do it. You will learn a lot from how they express ideas when the formality and 'good acting manners' of the text are lifted.

Listening

Get the actors to exchange their parts in a scene and play each other's characters, then get them to repeat it in their own words.

Communication

Sometimes actors have a clear idea of what is needed but are technically or emotionally blocked in doing it. Try out different ways of telling the story – through gesture or movement alone, for example. All acting is storytelling, and actors are unhappy when unable to tell the story they know.

EXERCISES

Unlike games, exercises are for developing skills needed in a particular role, and are mainly physical or vocal. We have looked at some for improving physical flexibility and now concentrate on vocal ones. Incorporate them in your warm-up.

Relaxation

This is essential for good vocal technique. Lie on the floor and relax without being floppy. Place your hands on your rib cage at its widest point and breathe in. Do not breathe heavily; inaudible intake is the aim. Now breathe out with a sigh. The air gone, you will feel a slight contraction of the rib cage. Repeat the exercise until you are comfortable with the rhythm, then control it by counting the breaths in and out. Being comfortable and relaxed is important, so do not go for any world records.

Controlling the sounds

Breathe in, and as you let the air out again make a slight 'er' sound, keeping it steady and listening to it. Experiment with the dynamics of it and of 'ah', 'ay' and the other basic vowel sounds.

The tongue

Basic to the actor's art is free and fluent communication with the audience, so clear speech is vital. Actors can have clarity problems through not using their tongues properly when they speak. They can develop tongue control with simple exercises on the consonants – 'l', 't', 'd','k' and 'g' – making sure that the tongue drops to the bottom of the mouth on each line.

Tongue-twisters and patter rhymes

Using these can bring great improvements in general enunciation. Gilbert and Sullivan lyrics are particularly useful. But keep in mind that the first aim is clarity, then dexterity then speed. No actor should sacrifice the first two to the last.

MEMORIZING

Learning lines, an actor's biggest burden, can be a problem, especially when home conditions do not favour it. Memory is a tool of the actor's trade and must be kept in training, e.g. by memorizing a short verse or prose passage every day. The brain quickly adapts to such learning. Watch for slow learners and help them when you can – by taking time to go over lines privately with them – but impress on your cast that rehearsal is *not* the time and place for memorizing.

VOICE TECHNIQUE

Let us return briefly to voice technique. A developed voice is a vital part of the actor's equipment, but it is not wise to go beyond the simple exercises outlined above without detailed study, and preferably some tuition.

WARM UPS - HALF AN HOUR WILL PRODUCE RESULTS!			
			DURATION
1	RELAXATION	- Actors lie on floor and focus on ceiling - Gently rise and stand with feet apart - Roll head gently forward and slowly rotate - Lift shoulders gently and drop - Work on each muscle-tense and relax	5 mins and rest
2	FLEXIBILITY	- Return to floor - Raise arms and legs gently in turn and control the timing of this - Keeping feet on ground raise torso with arms behind head - work on hands and feet joints - shake out all joints	5 mins and rest
3	WORKING TOGETHER	- Stand in circle. Play simple party games passing and catching to build concentration - Put actors in pairs or small groups and use games which develop awareness of each other	5 mins and rest
4	BREATHING	- Return to floor - exhale all breath and let lungs fill, then expel to controlled count (10-15 is enough) - Add pitched notes to this prefacing open vowels with 'M' consonant to open resonance	5 mins and rest
5	VOCAL WARM-UP	- Relax jaw and work on tongue flexibility - use tongue twisters and rhymes for agility (should be learned) - Sing simple rounds and catches focussing on volume control	5 mins and rest

IMPROVISATION

This is a useful tool, especially in rehearsal where the formalities of text or production are inhibiting to performers.

WHAT DO WE NEED?

The basics are simple: actors, time, space and a subject. Just as an orange crate is an improvised chair, so the actor needs something with which to work. Don't expect your actors to create something out of nothing.

WHAT ARE USEFUL SUBJECTS?

The simplest subjects give the actor most scope. Your aim is to use imagination to investigate a particular subject. Avoid detailed or elaborate scenarios and let the actors bring any additional complexity to the subject they want.

HOW LONG SHOULD AN IMPROVISATION LAST?

As long as it's useful. If it begins to flag, re-direct it with a new idea or a change of details. If improvisations are successful, try adding new ideas to them to extend their range.

WHAT'S IN IT FOR A DIRECTOR?

An improvisation shows you what your cast feel they *can* do or what they should do. Don't worry if the dialogue becomes repetitious or wild. The cast are trying to express what they feel.

HOW MUCH CONTROL SHOULD I HAVE?

A lot. Keep a close eye on the sequence as it develops and be ready to call a halt if you think things are getting dangerous. Don't use improvisations if you normally have problems disciplining your cast.

ARE THERE ANY RULES?

Games, exercises and improvisations are uncharted territory. Fooling about, showing off, and anti-social behaviour are out of order unless the whole group is prepared to take it. Improvisations should not be performances: control actors who use them as cabaret spots.

CHAPTER 9

PERIOD PLAYS AND CLASSICS

These are among the most exciting forms of theatre for actors and directors, and though they present problems they should be encouraged. The particular skills they demand are within the range of any actor, but the plays need a longer rehearsal time than modern plays.

WHAT IS A 'CLASSIC'?

For present purposes we may say that a period play is one set in another era but not written in it, while a classic is written for and about the society it depicts.

A classic makes great stylistic demands on the production team and must be done well to succeed at all. Audiences are largely familiar with such plays and will have expectations. Still, they are within the scope of non-professionals when approached with imagination, dedication and integrity.

WHAT IS SO DIFFERENT?

A contemporary play must convince an audience inhabiting the same world as its characters. A period or classic work must plausibly present a time and place in the past. Generally, period plays are in language that the audience can understand, but most classics, in prose or verse, are in an archaic speech, similar to ours but with barriers to comprehension that must be overcome in performance. Both period and classical plays need costumes, settings and movements different from those of modern life. These are not just problems but challenges to director and actors.

BUDGETING

Unless you plan to update a classic (by definition you cannot update a period piece) your budget will need a special profile in all the visual areas – sets, costumes, wigs, props, lighting – simply because period objects are harder to get than modern ones. An imaginative director and designer can solve these problems and need not be tied by a classical play's period. If they wish to stay faithful to the period they must be ready to pay for it.

ACCURACY

Some directors are famous for the skilled re-creation of past times through movement and gesture. That skill rests on detailed research and expert guidance. The alternative with a classic is to 're-invent' the period. The danger in being too faithful to a period is that actors may lose the play in trying to recreate period gesture and movement. Better to take only what you need from a period rather than create the period and slot the play into it.

THE DIRECTOR'S TASK

The director of a classic must, as with any play, decide on its meaning and how to convey it to an audience through speech, gesture and movement on stage. Whatever the concept it must be put across by these theatrical means, so the director must be able to communicate his understanding of all this to his team.

Actors can be intimidated by difficult language, and by complex explanations. They are doers, and will be frustrated and confused by directions that do not lead to something being performed. Be sure of what you think and communicate it simply. End with instructions rather than opinions.

Classics can get bogged down by static, wordy presentation. You must keep the stage and actors alive throughout, which means a strenuous time for you. Avoid long discussions, work on your feet whenever possible and keep your cast active. If you wish to concentrate on a particular section give the actors a rest, but avoid long breaks in the session.

Many period and classic plays offer the possibility of highly imaginative visual staging. Study your actors in the space, and use all your resources. This means knowing your script well enough to be able to watch the play instead of reading it.

ACTORS' PROBLEMS

Classical and period plays generally present greater technical and interpretive problems than modern ones, so be ready to help the actors at every point. At the same time try to be sure that you are directing them further into the play, not reinforcing barriers of unfamiliar language, values and acting conventions.

PERIOD MOVEMENT

All movement on stage must help to tell the story, but classics and period plays present problems because movement styles have changed radically in the past fifty years. Remind your actors of this and incorporate it when it is useful.

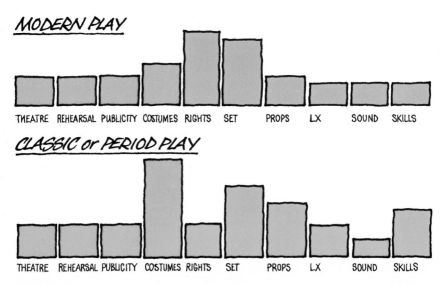

MODERN PLAY

THEATRE REHEARSAL PUBLICITY COSTUMES RIGHTS SET PROPS LX SOUND SKILLS

CLASSIC or PERIOD PLAY

THEATRE REHEARSAL PUBLICITY COSTUMES RIGHTS SET PROPS LX SOUND SKILLS

When bowing the actor is balanced, in full control and keeps eye contact with his colleague. The whole action is open and can be 'read' by the audience.

The actress prepares for a difficult curtsey while the scene continues, but maintains eye contact to 'stay in' the scene. Her hands are poised and her back straight for the next sequence.

PERIOD GESTURE

Gesture in period and classical plays can vitalize and illuminate if used sparingly, but can be fussy and tedious if used indiscriminately. It must be theatrically useful rather than just decorative, *growing out of* an actor's performance, not simply applied to it. Look at paintings of the period you are presenting. Many depict highly theatrical scenes and can show actors the power of gesture in such plays.

Here a complex body shape has been carried through into a highly characteristic use of the fan.

This actor is not really controlling the 'prop'. It will move and distract the audience.

Intensity of feeling has carried the actress with it. A clumsy rise has damaged a convincing scene.

The wide angle of the cloak is excellent. The actor uses costume to lend formality and conviction to a stylized gesture — and he won't trip over it when he exits!

REHEARSAL CLOTHES

To develop the movement and gesture needed for a particular period the actors must spend as much time in costume as possible. Money and the work of other departments will not permit you the actual costumes until the very late stages of rehearsal but you can, and must, have good rehearsal clothes that give the actors the feel of the period costumes in question. For women practice skirts are essential, and a basic one will serve any period. Period accessories – bustle, crinoline, bum-roll and so on – may be added. If women will be tightly corseted in the play ask the wardrobe department for appropriate corsets or a good dummy corset. They will co-operate if they have time, so ask well before rehearsals start. If large hats are to be worn they can be mocked up from old hat shapes or cardboard. If men will be wearing heavy overcoats ask them to rehearse in heavy overcoats that give some feel of weight and length. Shoes are always difficult, but an attempt should be made to find appropriate footwear at the start of rehearsals. At least discourage actors from wearing casual ones, trainers or sports shoes. Elaborate ruffs, collars and cuffs should also be simulated. They can get in the way in intimate contacts, so actors should get used to them.

PERIOD WIGS AND MAKE-UP

Wigs and some limited make-up are helpful to the total visual period effect. Without them costumed actors seem to be in fancy dress. Use them to unify the visual element in the production, but consult with the designer before deciding on specifics.

Actors often rightly resist elaborate make-ups, partly because of the time needed to apply them and partly because they seem like masks that will obstruct the actors in expressing what they want to play. Tell your actors at the start of rehearsals how they will look and show them finished designs. Copies of these are useful in the rehearsal room for checking movement problems caused by costumes, and for keeping actors aware of the overall effect being sought.

PERIOD COSTUME

To re-create plausibly the era in which a period play is set detailed research is necessary. You must know precisely the period that concerns you.

Good costumes are important here, and *the actors must feel right in them.* Women especially need the correct corsets and underwear. Unless it is a very static production the effect you want will be badly impaired by actors wearing modern underclothes. Any strong movement or gesture will betray the surface nature of the costumes.

In classical plays total accuracy is less important, and very expensive. It's better just to create an appropriate period atmosphere.

Remember that hired costumes, made for another production, may look quite wrong.

EXPENSE

The high cost of hiring costumes and wigs puts many groups off period and classical plays. If you go for a total period look it will be expensive, and your budget must be adjusted accordingly. Cutting corners will only mean shabby, ill-fitting costumes, and wigs that make the actors look foolish. One advantage of many classical plays is that they can be played on one set that serves all locations, which saves a little money.

IMAGINATION

An imaginative team can create exciting images from quite meagre resources, using ordinary materials to mount a visually elaborate production. As yours is unlikely to run for as long as a major commercial one you could benefit from this by creating for it original costumes that do not have to last. You must be aware of the materials available and detailed research can help with your imgaginative ideas. Only silk looks like silk; a substitute painted taffeta or calico will disappointingly fail to hang or move properly. But if the point of silk is to indicate opulence then you can achieve that with cheaper fabrics using paint, dye and trimmings. This approach makes for much more exciting work in wardrobe and props departments than does merely ironing hired costumes or finding props and decorations that 'will do'.

LANGUAGE

The director of a classical play must be able to help the actors understand its language well enough to convey character and action. You must be clear about the precise meaning of words in the script. Some words change their meanings over the centuries, and your concern is with what they meant *when they were written*. The dangerous words in a classical text are those that director and actors do not question. When preparing the play for rehearsal use footnotes and glossaries to help you understand the author's meaning, and check any still-doubtful words in an etymological dictionary of the kind that gives past usages.

Actors or directors who think precise meanings are irrelevant are in the wrong business, for everything on a stage must have meaning. Vagueness will confuse the audience and defeat the storytelling. Language in a play is vital to the story, characterization and action, and audiences know when actors are parroting speech they do not understand. Actors must not only understand the language, but also you must show them how to help themselves by controlling it. They should feel comfortable with their lines, not terrified by them.

VERSE PLAYS

Verse plays make great demands on all of the actors' skills, and the director must work closely with them on content, meaning and style. Allow time for this in your rehearsal schedule. However experienced, an actor needs time to train for the demands of a particular play.

Each line in a verse play has a rhythm formed with stressed and unstressed syllables. Thus the iambic pentameter:

Unvaried, the sound pattern above would soon become monotonous and sound artificial. Once actors are clear about the basic rhythm they must play with its stresses to find the 'music' that best expresses the play's various happenings. The basic rhythm should be seen as a skeleton on which flesh can be put. Your line could well start:

```
The quál i tý of mér cy ís not
stráin'd
```

```
The quál i ty of mér cy ís nót
stráined
```

Note the last word's single stress. Printed in full ('strained') it is spoken with two syllables but it should not be overstressed ('strain-ed'), a distracting effect that reduces intelligibility in rapid speech. The extra syllable should be marked with a weak stress but not made prominent.

Encourage your actors to move across the verse when speaking it. Unless a line ends with a stop do not give it a downward inflexion or pause before going on. Work towards the end of the line.

Proper breathing is important in speaking verse. Once the basic meaning and style are established the actor should give the lines as much energy as possible and not 'mark' too much.

THE WITS

[SCENE IV] — *NB LAST SCENE!*

'*Enter* Thrift, Snore, Mistress Snore, Queasy, Ginet.' — WHERE? FROM

Ginet. To him Mistress Snore; 'tis he has kept
Your husband from his bed so long, to watch
Him for a church robbery. — MOOD?

Mistress Snore. Ah, thou Judas! I thought what thou'ldst
come to!

NB STRENGTH OF OATH HERE

Remember the warrant thou sent'st for me
Into Duck Lane, 'cause I call'd thy maid trot,
When I was fain t' invite thy clerk to a
Fee-pie, sent me b' a Temple cook, my sister's sweetheart!

MEANING? WATCH PACE — REMIND AUDIENCE — NOT TOO FAST.

Queasy. Nay, and remember who was brought to bed
Under thy coach-house wall, when thou denied'st
A wad of straw, and wouldst not join thy halfpenny
To send for milk for the poor chrisom!

TEMPO? MAKE DIFFERENT FROM SNORE'S — A PHYSICAL WRONG

Snore. Now you may sweeten me with sugar-loaves
At New Year's-tide, as I have you, sir.

∥ VICTORY HERE

DON'T LET PACE DROP HERE

'*Enter* Thwack, Pert, Meager, Engine.' SAME DOOR?

Thwack. We'll teach you to rob churches. Slight here— TO FRIENDS TO DOOR
after
We of the pious shall be afraid to go— BACK TO DOOR NB VERSE — keep the delivery energised.
To a long exercise for fear our pockets should
Be pick'd. Come, sir, you see already how UK rhythms to stop gabbling
The neighbours throng to find you. Will you consent?
'Tis but a thousand pounds apiece to these
Two gentlemen, and five hundred more t' Engine.
Your crime is then conceal'd and yourself free.

SPEECH NEEDS TWO MODES ① TO DOOR ② TO FRIENDS.

Meager. No, he may choose, he'll trust to th' kind-
hearted law.
Pert, Let him, and to dame Justice too, who though
Her Ladyship be blind, will grope hard, sir,
To find your money-bags.
Engine. Sir, you are rich; besides, you know what you
Have got by your ward's death. I fear you will
Be begg'd at court unless you come off thus. — PROPS.
Thrift. There is my closet key. Do what you please.
Engine. Gentlemen, I'll lead you to it. Follow me. —

NEEDS INNER AREA LOCKED

SETTING

Most period plays call for a small number of naturalistic settings, and the problem here is how to create the required locations convincingly within one's technical and financial resources. The classic, epic or history play has quite different needs and possibilities that both director and designer must recognize for financial and artistic reasons.

THE UNIT SETTING

This setting fills the whole stage and, with minor adjustments, serves for the entire play. Based on theories of how Elizabethan plays, with their multiple locations, were performed, it offers a convenient and economical way of staging a multi-location piece.

Its advantages are that:
■ once erected it can stay up, unchanged, so it keeps its finish better than sets subject to dismantling and altering
■ it gives visual unity to plays that might become scrappy and confused.

Its disadvantages are that:
■ the audience will see the same picture all evening, so ingenious minor changes are needed to disguise that

■ it must look solid and permanent, which may mean expert building
■ it will need skilful lighting for the changes of mood and atmosphere that the play demands.

THE MULTIPLE SETTING

In this setting, perhaps derived from medieval guild theatre, one part of the stage is permanently allotted to each location, so the audience may at any point see all the play's locations simultaneously. Commonly used in very sophisticated productions, it can powerfully point up a play's internal contrasts or similarities. Visually it can be exciting, lending an almost fairground atmosphere to an otherwise sombre and colourless play.

Its advantages are that:
■ it is visually rich
■ it dispenses with scene-changes and on-stage crew so is well suited to open-stage productions
■ it is economical, one or two well-chosen objects serving for a whole built unit.

Its disadvantages are that:
■ it needs very careful use, with a clear, pointed acting style
■it can become confused and messy unless carefully controlled by lighting.

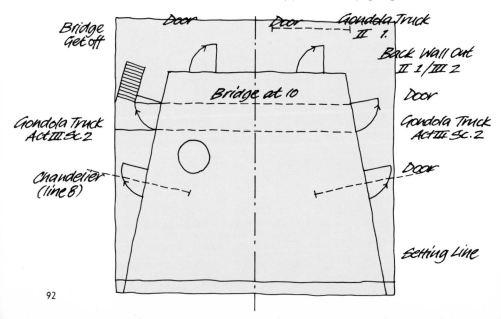

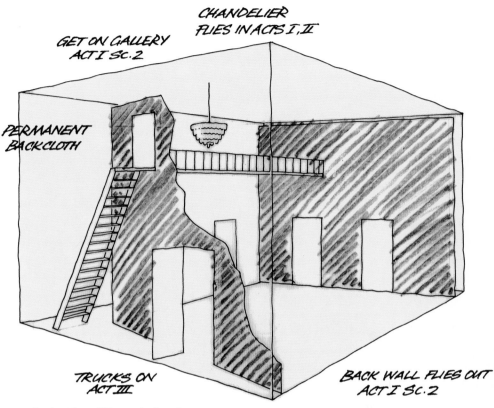

A unit setting: additions and subtractions create five locations.

MUSIC

Music can enhance any production. You may play it to amuse the audience during scene changes or to introduce or end your play, but it can also be used to elicit a particular audience response. It is integral to many classical plays, so you must decide how to go about this. If you want live music and your cast cannot play it you will have to hire musicians. *If the cast are playing and/or singing give them maximum rehearsal time from the earliest date.* Musicians and their work must be incorporated into the rehearsal schedule. If you are going to use recorded music give yourself plenty of time to choose it – and remember that you will have to pay a performance fee.

PROGRAMME NOTES

These can be useful or destructive. Do not tell your audience what you have 'tried' to do; it sounds apologetic. If your play has been done unconventionally write briefly about how *you* see it, not how you want the audience to see it. Many programmes include details of the play, its author and the ideas expressed in it. Be sure to know exactly what is going into the programme before it goes to print.

CHAPTER 10

BUSINESS REHEARSALS

You will have to give much attention to getting actors to appear relaxed and proficient in performing various activities. Allocate some time for this.

WHAT IS BUSINESS?

In the theatre 'business' means any on-stage activity by an actor, relating to another actor or an object, aimed at producing a specific effect.

HOW TO REHEARSE BUSINESS

When the basic action of a scene is established you can isolate areas relating to specific effects and allocate rehearsal time for working on them. If business is with props get them as soon as you can and work with them and the actor until they are 'user-friendly'. It is best to do this fairly privately. Working out such details in public can cause feelings of inadequacy and undermine confidence. When actors have business together call them separately so that they may get things right without feeling under pressure from each other, or that they are holding up rehearsals.

THE BEST TIME

Business rehearsals are most useful when a scene has been blocked but its final shape not yet settled. You may also have to devote time to business in technical rehearsals, in which case a business session in advance will save time and tempers during the technical

one. Where business depends on set or costume you may still be having problems well into production.

Rehearse before and after the dress rehearsal if necessary. Difficult business can be rehearsed before each show as a useful warming-up method.

DOORS REHEARSALS

Doors, the last things to appear on a set, are to actors the most important. Every entrance and exit must be gauged to bring the actor on or off at precisely the right time for the action and character. Bad doors can destroy these important moves, diminishing the actors or giving them nearly insuperable problems with their scenes. So *secure good practical doors*, and as soon as they are to hand set up a doors rehearsal.

How doors are used affects the flow of the whole production, and polishing entrances and exits to razor-sharp precision demands actors' undivided concentration, so call them to a stage where no one else is working (they must all know their lines if it is to work).

Before the doors rehearsal note every occasion on which a door is used, then go back to a convenient point in the scene before each one and use it as the starting point for rehearsing that occasion. Run the scene from that point, through the entrance or exit, then on past it a few lines. Repeat this until each use of a door fits into the flow of the scene. This is as important in serious plays as in farce or comedy.

 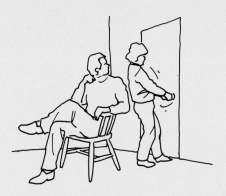

Actors must know the direction in which each door opens and be familiar with its mechanism – **how** it opens. Bad handling of doors will ruin the illusion and disrupt the play's rhythm and energy.

 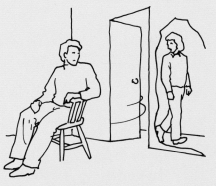

A door must be fully closed after an exit. When a quick change or re-entrance elsewhere follows, be sure that the stage manager closes the door for the actor.

Double doors need special handling; they must be opened and closed with both hands. If an actor is entering or exiting with props, have the stage manager 'page' the door.

COMIC BUSINESS AND TIMING

The essence of good comedy is timing. Every on-stage action must take no more time than is needed for it to fit easily into the play at that point, and a director holding up a production for business is in danger of losing the very response he is after. Vital to stage business is that the actor be well rehearsed and in control. Corners cut in rehearsal will show up badly in the performance.

It must be established at an early stage just what the actor will do and how long there will be for it. Some plays depend entirely on actors' timing to make them work, but these are within the scope of a cast prepared to work hard and be corrected a lot. Business needs an outside eye to gauge its effect, and as you become familiar with it you will see where it can be tightened up, edited, extended or otherwise changed.

Actors who have to perform business with objects during speech to which the business is apparently unrelated should have those objects from the very first rehearsal. Identify them and ask the stage manager to have them ready for the first session on that scene. Actors must be comfortable with things they have to work with and only practice allows that. When you choose a play be sure long before dress rehearsal that you can meet whatever business demands it makes.

BUSINESS WITH OTHERS

Sometimes actors must work together in what amounts to a 'routine'. Such tricky, sometimes dangerous passages need precise placing of the actors on stage and exactly the same movements each time. If they are to work the actors must share the load of each effect as a team. A play may have situations that are abnormal for the actors, but *as characters* they must carry them off easily and naturally. These can often be handled as business rehearsals, and there are technical solutions to most situations likely to arise.

The stage kiss is often left to the last moment to spare embarrassment, but the actors should kiss as soon as possible in rehearsal. Relax them with exercises, keep the mood light and remind them that the kiss is only play-acting. On-stage kissing looks more passionate the less mouth contact there is. Get the actors to embrace with their whole bodies and focus on downstage hands. Concentrating on another activity, they can make the audience believe in something rather more than a kiss. No real kissing should take place unless both actors want it. It can be unpleasant for an unwilling recipient.

Slaps and Hits are also difficult. Actors do not like hurting each other and have a residual concern about being seen as someone who 'does that'. Like the kisses they are only play-acting. Slapping on the face is easily simulated by positioning the actors so that the recipient's hands, hidden from view, make the slapping sound. The slapper takes all the weight out of the blow and carries it through. The recipient rides with it, moving imperceptibly before it lands.

A production with extensive violence needs a fight arranger or captain to ensure that the scenes are both realistic and safe.

Fluent body shapes and close contact create sensuality. Both backs are relaxed; tension weakens the sensual image.

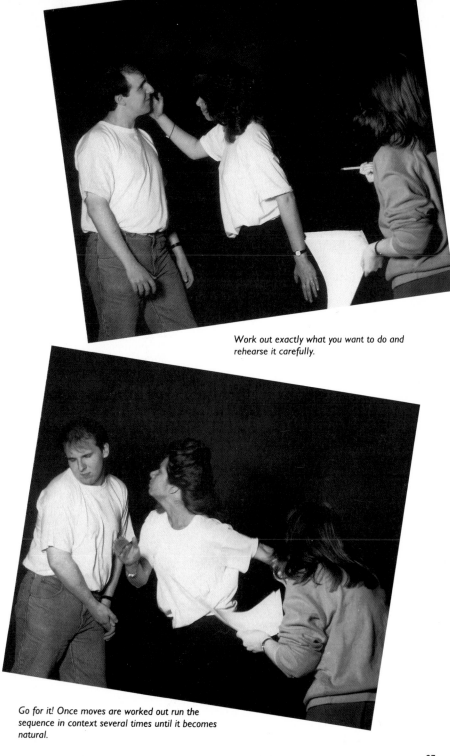

Work out exactly what you want to do and rehearse it carefully.

Go for it! Once moves are worked out run the sequence in context several times until it becomes natural.

CHAPTER 11

MUSICAL THEATRE

The added dimensions of music and dance mean extra hands on the production team – a conductor or musical director and a choreographer.

THE MUSICAL DIRECTOR

The musical director, usually also the conductor at each performance, works with singers, chorus, rehearsal pianists and orchestra on musical preparation and execution. Relations between director and musical director are important. Both want the best results in the limited time and each will have ideas about the other's province. Both must be satisfied if the production is to be a success.

MUSICAL SHOWS AND PACE

One of the most common faults in productions of musical shows is that the pace tends to flag. Three different media – speech, dance and song – are being combined in different ways cross the show and each of these makes specific demands upon your performers. A glorious singer may be a poor dancer, or a stilted deliverer of dialogue. How do you combined the three elements to give your production the apparent ease of all-round entertainment?

■ know where your performer's strength lies and shape the production accordingly. Avoid long dance routines for inexperienced performers, especially when singing or complex acting follows

■ try to achieve a balance in your staging so that the performer's strongest area emerges as such and weaker areas are played down
■ identify the flagging scenes of your production and run them as isolated sequences, simplifying where necessary and emphasizing the importance of keeping the sequence moving. Look particularly at your stage groupings. Poor contact between performers can often slow scenes down.

Dialogue scenes are all too often the weak point of musical productions and get too little rehearsal. Schedule proper time for your dialogue scenes and don't be put off by the feeling that your performers are principally singers and dancers. This is exactly why they will need *more* not less work on dialogue.

DIRECTOR
With SINGER

CONDUCTOR /
MUSICAL
DIRECTOR

PIANIST

STAGE MANAGER

CHOREOGRAPHER
With CHORUS

THE CHOREOGRAPHER

The choreographer works closely with the director to establish the exact mood and context of each musical number, then creates steps and dance routines, teaches them to the performers, stages the musical numbers and has a big creative role in shaping the production generally. The choreographer is interested in *all* the movement in the production and can be very helpful in solving movement problems. Good relations are vital here. Each is sharing the other's territory and must not fight over it.

TEAM WORK

This is essential in musical theatre. Meet with your musical colleagues and discuss thoroughly what you plan to do together and how to achieve it. Early consultation is the best basis for good relations throughout. Discuss in detail how you will rehearse the show. Each department must be sure of getting adequate rehearsal of its own contribution as well as its share of the common targets so that no one feels under unfair pressure.

CHOOSING THE SHOW

As when choosing a play your choice of a musical show will rest on your budget and resources, the material available, the likely audience and, of course, personal taste. As money is even more at stake than in an ordinary production you may be invited to direct a vehicle already chosen. But if you *are* involved in choosing, be sure that the choice is within your group's range. A good Gilbert and Sullivan troupe, to whom singing and acting are important, will have trouble with a dance musical like *Chicago* or *West Side Story*. Equally a dance troupe may not do very well with a romantic musical or operetta.

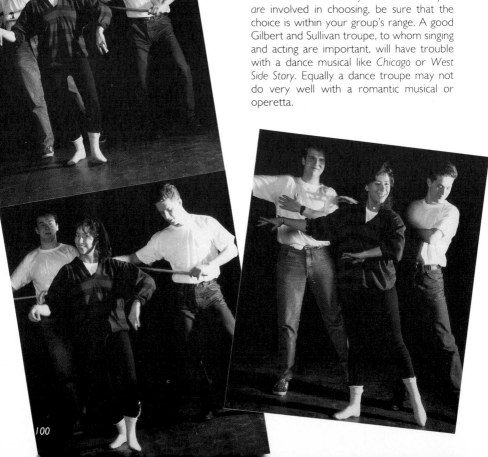

AUDITIONS

Auditions should be conducted by the director, the musical director and the choreographer. Plan together how you will hold them. To save time you should each hold separate sessions but attend each others'; the final choices will affect you all. *Musical auditions should be first.* At these the musical director grades candidates into those who are definitely wanted on the musical side, those who are not, and 'possibles'. The director then auditions for acting ability. It is important for you to hear the actors sing. Acting does not stop when a song begins, and performers must be able to interpret songs as well as sing accurately. Do not discount the non-singers. Many musical shows have good speaking cameos beyond the range of the vocalists.

When you have short lists for the various categories ask the performers to audition for the choreographer, then set to work casting.

Each of you will press your favourite choices but remember that you want a balanced team that can share the load of the show. If this is your first musical you may encounter actors who have long acting records with your group, but if they are unsuitable you must be firm. You have to work and achieve results with these people so you must have the best ones for the roles.

PRODUCTION: IOLANTHE

NAME: *JOHN BROWN*

ADDRESS: *24, GREENSTREET, BLACKROCK*

TELEPHONE (Home) *463712* (Work) *555155*

SINGING

Trained/untrained

Soprano/Mezzo/Tenor/Baritone/Bass

Range: *Fb2 – E4*

Voice type: Operatic/Light/Folk

Soloist/Chorus

ROLES POSSIBLE *LORD CHANCELLOR: STREPHON*

ACTING

Audition speeches

(1) *BLESS THE BRIDE : clear, light voice - carries - good projection*
(2) *IMPORTANCE OF BEING EARNEST: Rather mannered - but gets meaning across.*
(3) *STREPHON - O.K. - could do it with some work.*

DANCING *Very Good*

AVAILABILITY *Total*

OTHER COMMENTS *Rather lightweight but certainly soloist potential*

ACTION *Offer STREPHON if a...*

TUESDAY NOV. 9: COMMUNITY CENTRE		
PRODUCTION	MUSIC	DANCE
7.30 - 8.30 CHANCELLOR, PEERS CHORUS. ACT I with piano	7.30 - 8.30 PHYLLIS & STREPHON DUETS	7.30 - 8.30 LADIES CHORUS ACT I
8.30 - 9.15 NIGHTMARE SONG with piano	8.45 - 9.15 LADIES CHORUS ACT I	8.30 - 9.30 PHYLLIS AND STREPHON DUETS
9.15 - 10.00 LADIES CHORUS ACT I	9.15 - 10.00 FAIRY QUEEN all music	9.30 - 10.00 PEERS & CHANCELLOR ACT I
8.30 - 9.15	Fittings	MEN'S CHORUS
9.30	Fittings	PRINCIPALS AS AVAILABLE

Note how the same items are got ready, rehearsed and polished across the evening, to focus attention and aid preparation.

REHEARSALS

Rehearsals for a musical show are lengthy, tiring, and sometimes frustrating. They are also exciting and comradely, a time for abilities to be not just tested but extended. The show will take over your life. Even if you are able to rehearse the whole thing in a concentrated period you will have little time for anything else. A director's high level of activity in the last few rehearsals of a play will be more or less your level *throughout* the mounting of a musical show. Try to stay fresh for each rehearsal by being well prepared and having limited targets. Allow as much time as you can for the rehearsal period to combat stress.

Schedule the work so that the music is learned and prepared before rehearsals start. You and your choreographer can do nothing with performers still unsure of the music. The music learned, start work on production. As the musical numbers will take up a lot of stage time the blocking can be done quickly. Divide the rehearsal time two-to-one with the choreographer, in your favour. Once scenes are blocked, share the time equally. Attend the setting rehearsals of dances and musical numbers, then give the choreographer sessions to work in detail. When you feel that music and dances are well enough rehearsed start assembling the show in scenes and sections. Try to work with the chorus on at least one session per week at first. You may feel that your role is merely consultative, but your time will come; meanwhile prepare the technical areas of what will be a complex production.

TRAINING

Probably your performers will not be professionals but dedicated amateurs, to whom musicals appeal because of their highly social nature and the excellence of professionals, which can appear deceptively easy. Whatever the show your group must be trained. A Gilbert and Sullivan piece, say, in which thirty amateurs must act in unison, needs patient drilling rather than rehearsing. Whatever talent performers showed in audition must be developed to keep pace with the production. Make time especially for the vocal training. A decent teacher can improve any voice, which is good for the show and for future ones.

UNTRAINED VOICES

These are what most of us have, and they are not suitable for certain kinds of music. Singers can do themselves serious damage by overusing their voices or singing with no clear understanding. The untrained voice is not to be confused with the natural voice.

MICROPHONE TECHNIQUE

Though disdained in some traditional circles the microphone allows easy, unforced singing, but you need the best equipment and operators. Sound technology is now very sophisticated, and accounts for ten per cent of a professional musical's budget. Like lighting, sound must be designed, whether there are two microphones or twenty.

Save cost by placing microphones for maximum coverage. If they are in the conventional (concealed) footlight position make sure that your singers are covered across the stage. There must be no sound 'dips'. Ensure when blocking that songs are sung upstage of the microphones to keep singers' voices to the fore.

An audience watches the singer, not the mike – and the song sounds better.

A mike too close to the mouth looks awkward and distorts the sound.

LATE REHEARSALS

As production goes ahead you will see where the show's parts are not knitting together. Consult with your colleagues and ensure that the final weeks of rehearsal attack that problem rather than securing separate areas of excellence. The problems of musical theatre are such that it may be best to run the piece as often as possible until all are secure in what they are doing – and what you are not doing becomes clear.

PIANO RUN-THROUGHS

These are production rehearsals aimed at spotting and ironing out problems that arise in performance. Consult with the musical director on what is needed and ask musical staff to restrict notes and comments to specific periods of the rehearsal. Run each act right through and take notes. Give the cast your notes and take time to make necessary corrections. Any extra time can be given to music. If there is none ask the conductor to set up a separate rehearsal.

ORCHESTRA REHEARSALS

The arrival of the orchestra signals to everyone that real performances are close. Adrenalin flows and tempers rise. Any rehearsal involving the orchestra is con- trolled by the conductor, who may run it against the shape of the show. Find out beforehand how it will run, then sit back. You can learn a lot from a rehearsal that you do not control. It may depress you, but do not despair. Make notes and watch the

production's overall shape. It may now seem out of your control, but you can recover lost time through carefully judged notes. Once the performers are confident musically they will be eager for production notes again.

HOW BIG AN ORCHESTRA?

The size of your orchestra will depend on the scoring for the piece, your budget, how big your theatre is and how big its pit is. In the end pit size will be the limiting factor. The pit must accommodate the musicians comfortably.

The orchestra must also be matched to your singers' abilities. An orchestra can create a wall of sound that kills on-stage sound, wip- ing out words and meaning. Work out the best sound for your show with the musical director, keeping in mind limitations of performance rather than the composer's intentions.

PIT PROBLEMS

The orchestra's arrival causes problems beyond merely having new people about. The musicians need adequate – and differ- ent – playing spaces for their various instru- ments, also well-lit stands, which must not interfere with overall power-supply demand nor with the carefully lit images on stage. Orchestral players work in difficult condi- tions and like rather more light than can be offered. Tell your electrician and production manager of the orchestra's technical needs well in advance. Help relations between pit and stage by introducing yourself to the musicians at your first joint rehearsal.

MUSICAL REHEARSALS

CIVIC THEATRE:	22 NOV.
7.30 - 10.30	
7.00	Ladies Chorus to wardrobe
7.15	Principals Act I to wardrobe
7.30	ACT ONE RUN THROUGH with piano and lights. (Ladies & Principals in full costume & make-up please)
8.30	BREAK
8.45	NOTES
9.15	ACT ONE RUN THROUGH

ORCHESTRAL REHEARSALS

Tues 29 Nov   7.30 - 10.30   Orchestra alone

Wed 30 Nov   7.30 - 10.30   Full Company with orchestra

Thursday 1 Dec   7.30 - 10.30
    Run ACT I with orchestra & all staging

Friday   2 Dec   7.30 - 10.30
    Run ACT II with orchestra and stage

Saturday 3 Dec   2.30 - 6.00
    FINAL REHEARSAL
    with orchestra, costume, and lights

PIT PROBLEMS

PROBLEM	SOLUTION
NO LIGHT IN PIT	CHECK ALL STANDS **BEFORE** REHEARSAL BEGINS
INSUFFICIENT LIGHT	HAVE LIGHTS ON DIMMERS TO BOOST
TOO MUCH LIGHT	DROP LEVELS WITH ORCHESTRA PRESENT
NO ROOM	POSITION INSTRUMENTS ACCORDING TO NEEDS eg. TROMBONES NEED MORE ROOM THAN TRUMPETS
TOO MANY PLAYERS	CHECK BAND SIZE & PIT SIZE **BEFORE** ORCHESTRA ARRIVES
PLAYERS WON'T FIT IN PIT	EXTEND PIT AT SIDES FOR DOUBLE BASSES OR PERCUSSION: TAKING SEATS OUT MEANS LOSS OF REVENUE. **ALWAYS** CHECK BAND ACCOMODATION IN ADVANCE
TOO COLD IN PIT	CLOSE ALL DOORS AND HEAT HALL **BEFORE** REHEARSAL
BAND TOO LOUD OR SOFT	ADD OR REMOVE DRAPES TO MUFFLE OR SHARPEN SOUND

Musicians are vital to a production and should not be a mere afterthought. Their workplace is the pit, so keep it clean, warm and comfortable and look after their needs.

DRESS REHEARSALS

These are team efforts that anyone may interrupt but should try not to. The scenic and costume demands of a musical production are such that interruptions interfere with that important department. Let the show run, even if it is falling apart, and use notes and whatever time you can get to correct failings.

TECHNICAL PROBLEMS

When you encounter these in technical rehearsals give priority to those affecting performers – scene and costume changes and props work. At a dress rehearsal the main problems will be with lighting or scenery, and you can sort these out later. In a musical production try never to interrupt a dress rehearsal. You may not get another, and the cast have conditioned themselves to get through it, not to be interrupted about details.

TIMING

Try to establish running times before going into the theatre. Cutting a show that looked good on the floor has a bad effect on performers. Also, you need running times to know how to allocate technical rehearsal time. Watch and time each scene, noting the proportions of speech, music and dance. This will allow you to share out the available time, settle on priorities and avoid the long, exhausting technicals that can ruin a good musical.

TIREDNESS

Actors in musical productions use their bodies more strenuously than they may have been used for years and in ways quite unlike everyday life. The intense concentration needed for singing, dancing and acting can be exhausting. Take care not to work your cast too long without breaks. If they are badly tired by the time you reach late rehearsals create an opportunity to give them a night or weekend off. *A relaxed and rested troupe will give a better performance than an exhausted one.*

MARRIAGE OF FIGARO

– Running times –

7.00 prompt	Overture
7.04	Act I (28 mins)
7.32	Scene change
7.35	Act II (60 mins)
8.35	Interval 20 mins
8.55	Act III (30 mins)
9.25	Interval 20 mins
9.45	Act IV (45 mins)
10.30	Curtain Down

CHAPTER 12

TECHNICAL AND DRESS REHEARSALS

These advanced rehearsals mark the point at which the whole production is assembled and ready to be performed. They also mark the final stages of your contribution. Now is when you need the ability to take decisions and think of several things at once. Everyone is under pressure. Try to work without imposing more.

'TECHNICALS'

At technical rehearsals the work of the non-acting members of the group is brought together and got ready for performance. Everything that the performers will see, touch or wear must be completed and present at a technical.

PREPARATION

In the days approaching technical rehearsals make time to consult with all technical departments. Earlier they would have come to you, but in this period of pressure they will be loath to leave their workshops. Find out what problems they are having and, with your production manager, anticipate and rectify any others before the technical.

WHAT KIND OF TECHNICAL?

If technical activity accompanies action – say preparing and eating food, erecting a tent – you must run the whole sequence. But try to avoid this and go for a 'cue-to-cue' technical. Divide the play into short sections centred on technical or business effects, allowing time for the stage manager to instruct 'stand by' (get ready), then 'go' (complete the effect). In this way any production should be technically rehearsed in three hours unless special effects from machines are needed. Brief colleagues at a production meeting on how you want to do the technical. Never try to turn one into a dress rehearsal.

ASSEMBLY

A technical rehearsal is like a production line. Various components, made to highest standards, are assembled into an efficiently functioning whole. All departments should be represented by people to watch mainly their own contributions and report back on problems. Remember to thank your colleagues and congratulate them on things that work.

DIRECTORS AND SOUND TAPES

Sound plays a part in most productions, either as background music or as sound effects. Effects are taped beforehand and played during the performance unless (for door slamming, doorbell ringing and so on) actor-operation is better. Brief the sound operator early in rehearsal on what music and effects you want and where they will be used. The operator will provide a selection and you can decide which of them you want and how long each cue should be. The operator will then compile these into a show tape. Listen to it with the operator in the auditorium before the first rehearsal, when volume levels and cue times will be set. These can be further adjusted in technical rehearsal. For best results work closely with your operator and allow him or her ample time. Some quite simple-seeming effects are notoriously hard to get right.

LIGHTING AND DIRECTING

After stage design lighting is probably a production's most important element. It determines visibility, concentration level, the focusing of particular actors, mood, atmosphere and overall impact.

Meet with your designer and lighting designer at an early stage and, using the model box, discuss your basic approach. When the play is blocked go through the whole script with the lighting designer, clarifying any particular 'states' and cues that you want for certain moments.

Encourage the lighting designer to use as few lamps as possible. The more you use the more time you need. When the lights are focused you and the lighting designer will create the play's lighting. The set should be completed at this session, apart from minor details, and you should have to hand any costumes that may raise problems in certain lighting states. Get someone to walk on stage at these rehearsals so that you can check visibility and be sure that the lighting covers the stage.

Be realistic about cues. Use the fewest necessary to get your effects. If a lamp needs refocusing let the designer work round it rather than waste precious time refocusing during the session. Keep the lighting designer posted on any blocking changes that occur after the briefing stage.

SPECIAL EFFECTS

Special effects calling for lights or pyrotechnics are dealt with by the lighting department, non-electrical ones by props or stage management. With an electrical or mechanical effect *safety is paramount*. Run it before letting actors near the stage, then explain to them how it works and what the safety considerations are. Actors can get carried away while performing, so be sure that your effects are actor-proof!

Run an effect as often as you can afford to before the technical. If it involves destroying the equipment, as with a flash effect, have replacements ready and allow time for the effect to be set up again.

PROPS AND TECHNICALS

All the production's props must be ready for the technical, which is to ensure that the cast can handle them – but is *not* for rehearsing business. The stage manager will have assigned a props manager with whom actors should be encouraged to deal directly to save time and allow changes to be made before dress rehearsals.

SETTING UP A TECHNICAL

Allow time for adequate lighting and sound rehearsals after the 'get-in' and 'fit-up' are completed, then give your team a break. Be sure that all relevant personnel will be ready when needed and call actors as per performance, in costume and make-up. Technicals are usually tiring, sometimes boring, so director and stage manager must collaborate in working out what will be achieved and how. You will be nervous, but try not to let that interfere with the work – and try not to lose your temper.

HOW LONG A TECHNICAL?

This depends on how long and/or complex the production is and how much time you have for it. Most shows can be given an adequate technical rehearsal in three hours. With your stage and production managers discuss the show's complexities from their viewpoints and rehearse accordingly.

RUNNING A TECHNICAL

Have an adequately-lit production table with note-pads and pencils set up at a point in the auditorium from which the whole stage is visible and share it with the lighting designer and anyone else who is necessary. The stage manager will give all cues from the control desk and will be linked to the production table by a telephone or intercom (now quite cheap and a good investment). You may stop the technical but should do so for only two reasons: to get something right or to set up a difficult piece of business that has not been tried yet.

Encourage actors to stay in the auditorium when not taking part in a scene or changing costumes. Have a break in the schedule but ask the actors not to wander off; precious time is lost if actors cannot be found for their scenes.

CUE-TO-CUE

Opt, if you can, for the cue-to-cue technical discussed in *What Kind of Technical?* above. Properly planned, it will save time and tempers and keep actors busy and interested. A long, badly conducted technical can dispirit a cast for days. The cue-to-cue improves your chance of another dress rehearsal, always preferable to a long technical and one final dress rehearsal. It is also essential in musicals, when singers must not be kept hanging about in unheated theatres.

3.00	COSTUME PARADE
3.15	FLYING REHEARSAL
4.00	SCENE CHANGES WITH ACTORS
5.00	QUICK CHANGES
5.30	SET SOUND LEVELS
6.00	BREAK
6.45	TECHNICAL REHEARSAL BEGINS
8.00	BREAK (AFTER ACT I)
8.15	TECHNICAL CONTINUES
10.30	TECHNICAL ENDS

COSTUME BUSINESS

Hats are difficult for many modern actors; they are so rarely worn nowadays. Different ages had differing manners, so check period style books to be sure of correct business. Where to leave a hat and how to pick it up must be incorporated into entrance and exit business. An actor wearing a wig may have problems in donning or removing a hat naturally, and provision must be made for that.

Gloves and shoes that have to be removed on stage may present technical problems – buttons, laces and so on – which should be dealt with in detailed business rehearsal before the technical rehearsal. Remember that actors get hot on stage if there is a lot of business, so things like boots and gloves must fit properly. Costumes generally must be comfortable for actors who have to spend much time in them.

Taking off clothes on stage is a delicate matter, so avoid complete nudity unless you are sure it will neither embarrass the actor nor disappoint the viewer. While costume makes people look special, nudity makes them look ordinary. Asking an actor for nudity or near-nudity is asking a lot.

In plays that demand clothes being changed on stage ensure that they are all available in time to rehearse properly.

COSTUME BUSINESS

The actor must rehearse all costume business fully.

HATS – how to put them on and off without delaying the action.

GLOVES – must be handled with ease and familiarity.

SHOES – work with the real shoes as soon as possible to establish problems.

ASK the Wardrobe for these accessories.

TELL the Wardrobe what effect you want.

WORK with actors to make them easy with accessories.

N.B. Quick changes count as costume business. Rehearse them fully!

BUSINESS WITH PROPS

Any business with props can become an actor's nightmare and a director's catastrophe if not properly prepared. Actors have to work with all kinds of props, from pocket watches to stage coaches, and the only insurance against failure is letting the actor become completely familiar with the object. Actors must have total control of props on stage, so get them into rehearsal early and never do a run-through without them.

HANDLING PROPS

Props help an actor to make the story clearer or a character more convincing, so they must be used in ways that let the audience see them without being distracted by them. Much of this depends on how good the props are, but the actor's contribution is very important. Some actors are brilliant with props, others poor.Characterizations by actors who are not good with props should not be loaded with them.

Note how actors use props in rehearsal. Their belief in them is crucial. The props must be activated at certain points, then virtually forgotten, so an actor must act

rather like a conjuror with them, and familiarity is the first step to being convincing.

All this said, beware of over-using props. It can lead to fussy, unfocused acting affecting characters and situations. Watch, too, for actors depending too heavily on props to make up for superficial acting.

REHEARSAL PROPS

When it is not possible to have the actual performance props in the rehearsal room you will need adequate substitutes. If a prop has to produce a particular effect be sure the substitute can.

REAL PROPS

If your props department has been given adequate warning of your needs you should have your real props in late rehearsals and in run-throughs before going on-set. Objects on stage are to fulfil specific functions, so be sure you know what each one is to do and that it can be altered if necessary. Some objects may not do what you want of them. Consider them and the ideas carefully before putting them into the show.

DRESS REHEARSALS

These will give you some of your most nerve-racking moments as a director. This is partly because though still in charge you have gradually handed over direct control to other departments. You are now supervising from outside, and may be feel isolated from everything you have spent months working on. This is quite natural, but if you stop a dress rehearsal be sure it is because something is so wrong that the play cannot continue – not because you want to resume control.

WHEN?

A dress rehearsal should be attempted only when the whole play is thoroughly rehearsed and 'tech-ed'. This means adequate preparation and forward planning from the beginning.

HOW MANY?

How many dress rehearsals you need will depend on the production's complexity. Usually only two are possible – and they are adequate – but try for three so long as your notes after each one indicate that you are improving things, not just repeating them.

MOUNTING A DRESS REHEARSAL

Everything to do with the stage and costumes must be completed well beforehand so that safety can be checked. The actors must be in their dressing rooms half an hour before the session starts and are called as per performance. Allow time for notes after the rehearsal or provide for a notes session before the next one.

Very little of your production time is alloted to a dress rehearsal.

WEEKS	
1	PRODUCTION FIXED / DESIGN WORK BEGUN
2	ROUGH MODEL
3	
4	---AUDITIONS------ / FINISH DESIGN
5	CASTING / COSTUME WORK
6	SET BUILDING BEGIN
7	LIGHTING BRIEF
8	REHEARSAL
9	REHEARSAL
10	REHEARSAL
11	REHEARSAL
12	REHEARSAL
13	REHEARSAL
14	TECHNICAL / PLAYING
15	PLAYING / POST PRODUCTION

45

FRED: The trouble with you is tha[
a great deal more about yo[
ought to do.

ALG: While the problem with you
do not think at all.

(ALGERNON crosses to the
back the netting. The street
into the nearly dark room.
the fireplace and rings for th[

LXQ 12

LXQ 13
(visual

FXQ 4
(bell ring
quiet)

FRED: I sincerely hope that we shan[
over such a trivial matter.

ALG: I do not regard blackmail as [
matter.

FRED: Then clearly living in the coun[
distinctly blunted your sense o[

(SERVANT appears)

ALG: Morrison, will you please close
It is becoming morbidly dark in[

LXQ 14

switch

(MORRISON closes the curtains
men look at each other in silen[

FRED: Such a cheerful month Novembe[

ALG: Don't be such an idiot Freddie.

LXQ 15
(Electric light on)

(Morrison begins to light the lan[
goes to the wall and switches o[
electrolier).

ALG: Just the gas I think tonight.

LXQ 16
(Electric off)

(The electric is switched off)

PREPARING ACTORS

The cast must know their lines, their movements, what they will be wearing and when. Any trouble in these areas should have been spotted at late run-throughs and dealt with by firm notes to ensure that lines and blocking were learned. You should have ensured that characerization problems were not holding any actors up and done what you could. But some actors do not settle in their minds what they are doing until the dress rehearsal, so try to distinguish real confusion from nerves.

INTERRUPTING

Try never to interrrupt a dress rehearsal, certainly not for anything you can deal with in note form afterwards. You and your team are trying to assess the whole production, and unnecessary breaks make that impossible. If you *must* halt the session make sure that the actor has not changed costume; changing back uses up time.

Politeness is important. Let performers finish what they are doing. Cutting in on a speech or song disconcerts performers and makes them feel inadequate. If you have to stop for safety reasons try to avoid panic.

MAKING NOTES

The notes you make as you go along are very important to the production's development: Keep them clear, concise and in the form of instructions. Notes for actors should be simple and direct; they should not raise new ideas unless you are sure that the performers can carry them out. A new idea from the director at this stage can throw an actor totally.

Technical and stage management notes should also be clear and concrete. They should not ask for something new when a modification of the old is what you want.

When you make a note identify clearly for whom it is meant; this speeds up notes sessions. Some directors keep two notebooks, one for actors and the other for the rest. Few can do without written notes altogether. If there is someone to take notes

for you it will free you to watch the production even more closely.

Finally, keep your voice lowered at the production desk. Your comments could cause distress.

DIRECTOR'S SURVIVAL KIT

When you go into rehearsal take with you a current copy of the script, your notebooks, a supply of pens or pencils and a small electric torch. The last helps in making notes unobserved so as not to distract or upset the actors. Take some kind of refreshment with you but try not to smoke. In *no* circumstances should anyone have alcohol at a dress rehearsal. It blurs concentration and judgement, and can lead to accidents.

GIVING NOTES

You will have taken extensive notes during dress rehearsals, and at a note session shortly afterwards all notes affecting actors and others must be given to them. You can deal with the technical notes while the actors change, preferably by giving them all to the stage manager for passing on to the various departments.

After rehearsal let the actors relax but not 'switch off' before getting their notes. Offer general remarks at first, then move through the play chronologically, letting people go when you have spoken fully with them. Say something to each about his or her work and make all your specific notes instructions relating to line references. *Vary the tone of the session occasionally by asking what went wrong instead of telling the actor.* Make any negative comments firmly but politely and avoid tantrums or rows. Any harsh individual criticism of an actor should be delivered privately without sarcasm or anger. The point of notes is to give the team *positive* encouragement towards better work, not to make people feel inferior. Always emphasize the next time rather than dwelling on past failures. Before sending the actors away thank and encourage them. Notes are not worked on as constructively by a despondent cast.

CHAPTER 13

PERFORMANCES

At the end of dress rehearsals you must hand over to the cast and technical team the end result of all your work with them: the show. Attend performances whenever you can and enjoy the success you have helped to create. If you have useful comments give notes afterwards.

HANDING OVER

Many directors find it hard to hand over to the cast, feeling that they are now redundant. In fact you are still an important member of the team, but your role now is to support and encourage the actors. Avoid bullying them. Let them take charge of their performances. Trust is an important element in directing. Look realistically at what you have achieved and consider what lessons it offers for next time.

PEP TALKS

The cast will be used to your input and miss it if you withdraw completely. Stay in touch with them throughout the run and visit them before or after performances, encouraging them to maintain or improve their standards. Even if you have had disagreements they will want to know what you think. Be as positive as you can. Negative remarks are bad for morale, especially when actors tell each other about them.

NOTES TO AVOID

By this stage you should be a skilled diplomat, and the notes you give now must not make actors feel self-conscious. You should even arm them against any negative comment that may already have affected them. Avoid commenting on personal appearances. Get the costume supervisor to put right anything making an actor look foolish rather than criticizing how the actor looks. If there is a lapse of discipline you must have a full, accurate account before confronting the actor. Avoid notes based on hearsay. You cannot comment on what you have not seen. If an actor wilfully introduces changes detrimental to others or to the show itself ask him or her about it rather than going on the attack. Backstage harmony is vital to a good run.

Never accuse an actor of being drunk. You cannot prove it. But, if you think it is true take the actor aside and discuss it civilly. Replacing an undisciplined actor is more trouble than straightening one out.

NERVES

Most performers have nervous attacks before going on but you can get them to use that energy positively. Group sessions before the show can help to channel the nervous energy towards a good performance. Get the cast together before the half-hour call and work on some simple relaxation exercises. Old favourites from the rehearsal period will give the actors the feeling of working once more in a familiar not-too-demanding environment. Keep the sessions light, undemanding and short.

Be supportive of your cast and relax them further by discussing prosaic things rather than giving them more to think about. A rush of last-minute notes will distress any actor. Keep any such notes simple and few, and remind the cast how well they can do what they do and how much you want to see them doing it.

On no account offer tranquilizers or alcohol to calm nerves. They blur concentration and impede performance.

WARM-UPS

These help to divert actors' attention from the performance situation to the work to be done, but should also tone the actors up for performing. Be careful not to exhaust your cast before they go on, especially if they work during the day. *Special routines like fights or dances should be done before each performance to ensure safety and accuracy.* Provide rehearsal space for all this.

LAST-MINUTE PANICS

Any performer can panic just before the show, usually over a missing prop or costume, so be sure that everything the actors need is in place before the half-hour call *and stays there.* If you have staff to make up or dress the actors, have them call at appointed times that, if possible, suit the actors. Performers can usually improvise their way out of trouble, but you and your team must save them anxiety whenever you can.

TO SEE – OR NOT TO SEE?

That is the question on the first night, when you will be quite as nervous as the cast but without their outlet for anxiety. Deciding whether to watch or not can be agonizing, but you owe it to yourself and your colleagues to do so. Take notes if necessary – or if it helps you – and if you are *really* nervous stand at the back of the house or sit at the side; your nervousness could spoil the evening for others.

Attend as many performances as you can while you feel it to be useful but stop going if you get bored. You have seen more of the play than anyone, and perceptible boredom will affect the others' morale.

PRAISE – AND SYMPATHY

After performances – certainly after the last one – speak to everyone in the cast and team. General praise and thanks are part of the theatre but you must also comment specifically on individuals' particular contributions. Actors who have made mistakes or fluffed their lines will know it well enough; there is no point in making them feel bad. Offer your commiseration. They need their confidence restored for next time.

POST-PERFORMANCE PROBLEMS

Note clearly any problems you detect during the performance and afterwards discuss them quietly with your colleagues. Perhaps a cue needs to be moved or an effect retimed. If the change affects actors call them for an early rehearsal next evening to sort the problem out.

Performance notes on acting should be got to the actors before they play again. If you feel that the show is below its potential you must say so. Do not let the audience's acceptance stop you saying the show could have been better – if you can say how.

If a difference of opinion causes friction between cast members you must arbitrate, ensuring that the interests of the show come first. If a rebuke is in order deliver it gently and explain why the cause of it is not acceptable.

ASSESSMENTS

As the production nears its final performance you will have built up a backlog of reactions. Praise will have come from unexpected quarters; old friends will have disappointed you with over-critical reactions. Throughout all this keep a clear head about what is good and bad in the show and distribute praise, but be economical with blame. Quality control is your province, and constructive analysis is your tool.

TAKING CRITICISM

The show will be very close to your heart and you will feel protective about it and the cast. So you may be deeply wounded by any harsh criticism. Look behind the invective and sneers, which may conceal a reasonable argument worth listening to if you have angered someone. If there is no substance to the criticism ignore it; you have nothing to worry about.

RETROSPECT

After the final curtain of the last night you can look back and assess just what you achieved. You will be proud of much of it, but you must be realistic.

Your question now is not How good was the production? but Did I enjoy the whole thing enough to want to go through it again? Look back at the times that you did not enjoy and try to discover why. Consider how much you were prepared and how well you coped with unknown quantities. Do you now regret anything as a wrong direction? Did you fail to get certain results – or get results at the expense of morale and good relations? If there is a next time would you seek different solutions? Examine all this in conversation with a close production colleague or someone who will listen and comment objectively. And do not forget all the things that went right!

Dedication and hard work can bring out dormant talents, and directing can be done by anyone interested in theatre, people and team-work. The last is the key. A good director cannot be a one-man show.

Glossary

A

Anti-pros (US) see Front-of-House lights

Apron extension of stage beyond the proscenium

ASM assistant stage manager

Auditorium area in which the audience is accommodated during the performance

B

Backcloth cloth usually painted, suspended from Flies at the rear of the stage

Backing (1) cloth or solid pieces placed behind doorways and other openings on sets to conceal stage machinery and building (2) financial support for a production

Bar horizontally flown rod (usually metal) from which scenery, lighting and other equipment are suspended

Bar bells bells sounded in all front-of-house areas to warn audience that the performance is about to continue. Operated from prompt corner, and so usually written into prompt copy

Barndoor adjustable shutters attached to stage lights to control the area of light covered by a particular lamp

Batten (1) see Bar (2) piece of wood attached to flown cloth to straighten it and keep it taut (3) piece of wood joining two flats (4) a group of stage lights suspended over the stage

Beam light a light with no lens, giving a parallel beam

Beginners call given by deputy stage manager to bring those actors who appear first in the play to the stage

Bifocal spot spotlight with additional shutters to allow hard and soft edges

Black light ultra violet light

Blocking the process of arranging moves to be made by the actor

Board lighting control panel

Book (1) alternative term for the scripts (2) the prompt copy (3) the part of a musical show conducted in dialogue

Book flat two flats hinged together on the vertical

Booking closing a book flat

Boom a vertical lighting bar

Boom arch used to hang a lantern from a boom

Border flown scenic piece designed to conceal the upper part of the stage and its machinery or equipment

Box set setting which encloses the acting area on three sides. Conventionally in imitation of a room in which the fourth wall has been removed

Brace portable support for flats

Bridge walkway above the stage used to reach stage equipment

C

Call (1) warning given at intervals to technicians and actors that they are needed on stage (2) notice of the time at which actors will be required to rehearse a particular scene

Callboard notice board on which calls and all other information relevant to the production should be posted

Cans headsets used for communication and co-ordination of technical departments during a performance

Centreline imaginary line drawn from rear to front of stage and dividing it exactly in half. Marked as CL on stage plans

Channel a circuit in the lighting or sound system

Chase a repeated sequence of changing lighting states

Check to diminish the intensity of light or sound on stage

Cinemoid a colour medium or filter

Circuit the means by which a lantern is connected to a dimmer or patch panel

Clamp C or G clamps are attached to lights to fasten them to bars

Cleat fixing on the back of flats to allow them to be laced together (cleated) with a sash line or cleat line. Also a metal fly rail to which ropes are tied

Clothscene scene played before downstage drop or tabs, while a major scene change takes place

Colour call the list of coloured gels required for a lighting design taken from the plan of the lighting design

Colour frame holder for the colour medium or filter in front of the light

Colour Medium translucent filter material placed in front of lights to give a coloured illumination

Colour wheel in lighting, a device attached to lamps which, when rotated, charges the colour medium through which the light is shown

Come down (1) instruction to actor to move towards the audience (2) instruction to lower intensity of sound or light (3) end of performance; time when curtain comes down

Corner plate triangle of plywood used to reinforce the corners of a flat

Counterweights mechanical system used for raising and lowering flown scenery

Counterweight flying the system of flying scenery, lights etc., whereby the flown item is balanced by counterweights

Crossfade the practice of moving to a new lighting or sound effect without intervening darkness or silence: one effect fades out simultaneously with the new one's being brought into play

Crossover (1) the device on a sound system that routes the sound of the correct pitch to the correct part of the loudspeaker; (2) the space behind the stage setting or below the stage through which actors can get from one side of the stage to the other without being seen by the audience

Cue (1) verbal or physical signal for an actor to enter or speak a line (2) point at which an effect is executed or business takes place

Cue light box with two lights, red and green, which warn an actor or technician to standby (red) and then do (green) whatever is required of them. Ensures greater precision when visibility or audibility is limited

Cue sheet list of particular effects executed by one department in a production

Cue-to-cue rehearsal of technical effects in a production with actors. The scene is rehearsed in sections beginning with a cue for standby, and concluding when the effect is finished

Curtain call process of actors appearing at the end of the play to receive audience applause. Formerly actors were called before the curtain by the audience

Curtain speech out of character address to the audience by a cast member or participant

Curtain up (1) time at which a play begins (2) a call given to the company to warn them the performance has begun

Cut cloth vertical scenic piece cut to reveal more scenery behind it. Most common in musicals

Cutting list list of materials required for scenery and set construction together with the correct dimensions of the pieces

Cyclorama undecorated backing to a stage, usually semi-circular and creating a sense of space and height. Often some theatres have permanent or standing cycloramas which have actually been built. The term is always abbreviated to cyc

D

Dead (1) the point at which a piece of scenery reaches the desired position onstage (2) a redundant production or scenic element

Decibel dB the measurement of volume of sound

Diffusion (colour) used like a gel but to soften and spread the beam of light rather than to colour it. Also called a frost

Dim the process of decreasing the intensity of light onstage

Dimmers the apparatus whereby lights are electrically dimmed

Dip small covered hole in stage floor with electric sockets

Dock area at side or rear of stage where scenery is stored when not in use

Downstage part of stage nearest to audience

Dress circle also known as the circle. Area of seating above the stalls and below the balcony

Dressing items used to decorate a setting

Dress parade the final check of costumes before the first dress rehearsal. The cast parade each of their costumes in order before the Director and Costume Designer so that any final alterations can be made

Drop suspended cloth flown into stage area

DSM deputy stage manager

Dutchman (US) thin piece of material used to cover the cracks between two flats

E

Elevation a working drawing usually drawn accurately and to scale, showing the side view of the set or lighting arrangement

Ellipsoidal the type of reflector used in many profile spots

Entrance (1) place on a set

through which the actor may appear (2) point in the script at which an actor appears

Exit (1) the process of leaving the stage (2) point in the script at which an actor leaves the stage

F

Fader a means of controlling the output level of a lantern (lamp) or amplifier

False proscenium construction placed behind the real theatre proscenium for decorative or practical purposes

Fit-up installation of lighting, technical equipment and scenery onstage when coming into a theatre

Flash-out system to check whether the lights are functioning properly by putting them on one at a time

Flat scenic unit comprised of wood or stretched cloth applied to a timber frame and supported so that it stands vertical to the stage door. Door flats and window flats have these openings in them. Masking flats are placed at the outer edges of the acting area to disguise areas of the stage from the public

Flies area above the stage in which scenery, lighting and other equipment are kept. If whole backdrops are to be stored then the flies should be at least twice the height of the stage opening

Floodlights also called floods. Lights which give a general fixed spread of light

Floorcloth painted canvas sheets placed on the stage floor to give a specific effect

Floor pocket (US) see dip

Flown (1) scenery or equipment which has been suspended above the stage (2) flown pieces are any scenic elements which will be made to appear or disappear from view in sight of the audience

Fly the process of bringing scenery in and out of the stage area vertically

Flying (1) the process of stocking the flies (2) special effects whereby actors are suspended by wires to create the illusion of flying

Fly floor gallery at either side of the stage from which the flies are operated

Floats see footlights

Focusing the process of fixing the exact area to be lit by each light onstage

FOH Front-of-house. Any part of the theatre in front of the proscenium arch

Follow spot light directed at actor which can follow all movements

Footlights lights set into the stage at floor level which throw strong general light into performers' faces downstage

Fourth wall imaginary wall between audience and actors which completes the naturalistic room

French brace support for scenery fixed to stage

Fresnel type of spotlight with a fresnel lens which gives an even field of light with soft edges

Frontcloth see cloth

Front-of-House lights lights hung in front of the proscenium arch

Frost see diffusion

G

Gauze painted cloth screen, opaque when lit from the front, that becomes transparent when lit from behind. Often used at front of stage to diffuse total stage picture

Gel Colour medium introduced before light to alter colour of beam

Get-in/out (US) see fit-up process of bringing scenery into or taking it out of the theatre

Ghost a beam of light which inadvertently leaks from a light and falls where it is not wanted

Gobo (1) screen introduced before a stage light to give a particular image onstage (2) cut out shape that is projected

Green room general area in which cast and crew wait during performance

Grid metal frame from which all flying equipment is suspended

Groundrow raised section of scenery usually depicting bushes rocks etc.

Grouping (US) see blocking

H

Half half hour call. Warning to company given thirty-five minutes before performance

Handprop any prop handled by an actor, such as a handbag, walking stick, umbrella

Hanging attaching flying pieces to appropriate bars

Hook clamp the device that holds a lantern onto a bar

Hot lining the method by which lanterns, bulbs and cables are checked during rigging
House (1) audience (2) in opera, the entire theatre, and by implication, the company

I

Impedance a term for the electrical resistance found in a/c circuits, thus affecting the ability of a cable to transmit sound as electrical pulses. Measured in ohms
In one (US) see clothscene
Inset a small scene set inside a larger one
Iris a device within a lantern which allows a circular beam to be altered through a range of sizes
Iron a fire proof curtain that can be dropped downstage of the tabs in case of fire. Today it is usually made of solid metal and is electrically operated

K

Kill instruction to cease use of particular effect in lighting or sound

L

Ladder a ladder-shapped frame used for hanging side lights. It cannot usually be climbed
Lamp unit of lighting equipment
Lantern see lamp
Left stage left. That part of the stage to the actor's left when he is facing toward the audience
Leg cloth suspended vertically from flies and used to mask sides of stage and small areas within it
Levels (1) indicates intensity or volume of light or sound (2) raised areas onstage used for acting
Limes jargon for follow spots and their operators
Line drawings (US) see technical drawing
Linnebach projector used for projecting a picture from a gel or glass slide onto the set. Often used to give a shadow effect
Load in/out (US) see get in/out
Lose to turn off lighting or sound, or to remove an article from the set
Luminaire international term for lighting equipment. Not restricted to theatrical lighting

M

Marking (1) in use of props or scenery, the deployment of substitutes for the real object during rehearsal (2) in singing, a

means of using the voice with reduced volume and without vocalising extremes of register (3) any account of a role in which the full powers are not being used by the performer in order to save resources
Maroon a pyrotechnic giving the effect of a loud explosion
Mark out the system of lines and objects set on a rehearsal room floor to indicate the exact position of scenery and furniture. Marking out is the process of doing this
Mask to hide or conceal unwanted areas or machinery. Also used to describe one actor obscuring another unintentionally
MD musical director
Memory memory board. An advanced type of lighting control system where the required levels are stored electronically
Mezzanine area of seating above the orchestra and below the balcony. When a theatre has only a single balcony, first several rows are frequently designated the mezzanine
Mixer sound controls desk, used to mix and adjust levels of sounds from various sources

O

Offstage any backstage area not seen by the audience. Most specifically used to indicate the areas at the actor's right and left
OP opposite prompt. Stage Right (US Stage left)
Orchestra (US) see stalls
Out flying term for up
Overture (1) the music which begins a performance (2) a call to the actors and technicians that the performance is about to begin in a musical work

P

PA system the public address or any sound amplification system
Pack a number of flats all stored together
Pan (1) movement of lighting from side to side (2) used to describe water-based stage make-up (pancakes) (3) term (now nearly obsolete) to describe theatre sound installation
Parcan type of lantern which holds a par lamp
Patch border panel a panel at which the circuits governed by individual lighting dimmers can be changed
Perch lighting position concealed behind the proscenium

Periactus a tall, prism-shaped piece of painted scenery which can be revolved to show various phases
Pipe (US) see bar
Places please (US) see beginners
Platform (US) see rostrum
Plot (1) commonly used to describe the action of a play (2) any list of cues for effects used in the play
PM production manager
Practical any object which must do onstage the same job that it would do in life, or any working apparatus e.g. a light switch or water tap (faucet)
Preset (1) used to describe any article placed in its working area before the performance commences (2) also describes a basic lighting state that the audience sees before the action begins
Projector (US) see floodlight
Prompt copy fully annotated copy of the play with all the production details from which the show is run each time it is performed
Properties props. Any item or article used by the actors in performance other than costume and scenery
Props skip basket or cupboard in which props are kept when not in use
Props table table in convenient offstage area on which all properties are left prior to performance and to which they should be returned when dead
Pros proscenium arch the arch which stands between stage and auditorium. A pros arch theatre is a conventional theatre with a proscenium arch, usually without a forestage
PS prompt side. Conventionally meaning stage left, the term now refers only to the side of the stage in which the prompt corner will be found. In the US the PS is generally stage right
Prompt corner desk and console at the side of the stage from which the stage manager runs the show
Pyrotechnics any chemical effects used onstage or in wings to create lighting or special effects

Q

Quarter back stage pre-show call given twenty minutes before curtain up (ie. fifteen minutes before beginners)

R

Rail bottom or top batten of the frame of a flat

Rake the incline of a stage floor away from the horizontal; a raked stage is higher at the upstage end than at the downstage

Readthrough early rehearsal at which the play is read without action. Usually accompanied by discussion

Reflectors the shiny surfaces in the back of lighting equipment which help intensify the beam

Rigging the means of fixing lamps to appropriate bars before lighting a production

Right stage right. That part of the stage to the actor's right when he is facing the audience

Risers the vertical part of a stage step

Rostrum a raised platform sometimes with a collapsible frame used for giving local prominence to certain areas onstage

Run (1) the number of scheduled performances of a work (2) abbreviated form of run through

Runners a pair of curtains parting at the centre and moving horizontally

S

Saturation rig an arrangement of lights in which the maximum number of spotlights is placed in every possible position

Scatter the light outside the main beam of a spot

Scrim (US) see gauze

Seque musical term indicating that one number should go immediately into the next

Set to prepare the stage for action. To set up is to get ready. To set back is to return to the beginning of a given sequence

Shutter device in front of lamp to alter shape of beam

Single purchase counterweight flying system where the cradle travels the same distance as the fly bar's travel. The counterweight frame therefore occupies the full height of the side wall of the stage

Sightlines the angles of visibility from the auditorium

SM stage manager

Snap line chalk line, chalked piece of string which when stretched tight is used for making straight lines on stage

Special piece of lighting equipment whose main function is to perform a particular effect

Spiking see marking

Spill unwanted light onstage

Spot spotlight. Light giving a small circle of light, the dimensions of which can be precisely controlled by focusing

Stagger-run runthrough at which the production is pieced together, aiming at fluency but allowing for corrective stops

Stalls floor level area of seating in the auditorium

Strike instruction to remove any redundant or unnecessary object from stage

Super non-speaking actor not specifically named in the text

Swag curtains or tabs gathered together so they do not hang straight

Switchboard board from which lights are controlled

T

Tabs theatre curtains, most usually the House curtain

Tabtrack metal track on which the tabs run allowing them to open and close

Tallescope extendable ladder on wheels used in rigging and focusing lights and for minor corrections to flown pieces

Teaser short flown border used to mask scenery or equipment

Tech technical rehearsal at which all technical effects are rehearsed in the context of the whole production

Theatre in the Round acting area with audience on all sides

Throw in lighting, the distance between a light source and the object lit

Thrust stage type of stage which projects into the auditorium so that the audience can sit on at least three sides

Tilt the vertical movement of light

Tormentor (US) see teaser

Trap hole cut in stage and concealed by floor allowing access from below. Grave traps are usually double traps creating the illusion of a grave or pit. Once a common part of all theatres traps are now becoming increasingly rare

Trapeze single short hung lighting bar

Treads the flat part of stage steps

Truck movable cradle upon which scenery is placed to facilitate its movement

U

Upstage in a proscenium or thrust stage the area furthest away from the audience

W

Wagon (US) see truck

Walk-through rehearsals at which actors go through entrances, moves and exits to make clear any changes or alterations made necessary through change of cast or venue

Warning bells (US) see Bar bells

Ways the maximum number of combinations of channels on a lighting installation

Wings the sides of the stage concealed from the audience's view

Work-out in a dance or movement rehearsal, a vigorous session to prepare the body for specific work

Workshop any non-performing backstage area of a theatre

Workshop performance a performance in which maximum effort goes towards acting and interpretation rather than sets or costumes

Musical theatre special glossary

Andante walking space

Allegro happily, lightly

Allargando getting broader

Coda last section of music, often in a different tempo or mood

Cadence the resolving chords in music

Largo broadly

Lento slowly

Maestoso majestically

Presto fast

Aria solo, usually reflective in content

Duet musical number for two singers

Trio three singers

Quartet four singers

Ensemble (1) together (2) place in which all the characters all sing together

Finale (1) the end (2) by extension, a musical sequence which ends each act, often comprising different musical material but having an overall shape

MD musical director

Band parts the individual copies required by each player in an orchestra and containing only the notes for their particular instrument.

BIBLIOGRAPHY

Listed below are a representative selection of books for each of the titles in this series.

General

In the United States the Theatre Communications Group Inc. (TCG) (355 Lexington Avenue, New York, NY 10017. Tel: 212 697 5230.) has a publications department which publishes not only plays and books but also a monthly magazine of news and features called *American Theater*. It also publishes an employment bulletin for the performing arts called Art SEARCH.

In the United Kingdom Spotlight publish annually *Contacts*, a complete guide to British Stage, TV, Screen and Radio (42 Cranbourn Street, London WC2. Tel: 01 437 7631.)

Bentley, Eric *Theory of the Modern Stage*, London, 1968; New York 1976

Brook, Peter *The Empty Space*, London and New York, 1985

Brown, John R *Drama and the Theatre*, London and New York, 1971

Hoggett, Chris *Stage and the Theatre*, London and New York, 1971

Oren Parker, W L Smith, R Harvey *Scene Design and Stage Lighting*, London and New York, 1979

Stanislawski, K *An Actor Prepares*, London, 1981; New York, 1952

SUPPLIERS AND STOCKISTS

Costume and Make-Up

Barton, Lucy *Historic Costume for the Stage*, Boston, 1938

Barton, Lucy *Period Patterns*, Boston, 1942

Corson, Richard *Fashions in Hair*, London, 1985

Corson, Richard *Stage Makeup*, New York, 1960

Cunnington, Phillis and Lucas, Catherine *Occupational Costume in England*, London, 1967

Directing a Play

Berry, Cicely *Voice and the Actor*, London and New York, 1974

Hagen, Uta and Frankel, Haskel *Respect for Acting*, New York, 1980

Hodgson, John and Richards, Ernest *Improvisation*, London, 1978; New York, 1979

Nicoll, A *The Development of the Theatre*, London and New York, 1966

Willett, John *The Theatre of Bertolt Brecht*, London, 1983; New York, 1968

Lighting and Sound

Bentham, Frederick *Art of Stage Lighting*, London, 1980; New York, 1968

Burris-Meyer, H and Mallory, V *Sound in the Theatre*, New York 1979

Moore, J E *Design for Good Acoustics*, London, 1961; New York, 1979

Pilbrow, Richard *Stage Lighting*, London and New York, 1979

Reid, Francis *Stage Lighting Handbook*, London, 1982; New York 1976

Stage Design and Properties

Govier, Jacquie *Create Your Own Stage Props*, London and New York, 1984

Leacroft, Richard and Helen *Theatre & Playhouse*, London, 1984

Molinari, Cesare *Theatre Through The Ages*, London and New York, 1975

Oren Parker, W L Smith, Harvey R *Scene Design and Stage Lighting*, London and New York, 1979

Stage Management and Theatre Administration

Baker, Hendrik *Stage Management and Theatre Craft*, (3rd Edition), London and New York, 1981

Crampton, Esme *A Handbook of the Theatre*, London and New York, 1980

Gruver, Bert *The Stage Manager's Handbook*, New York, 1972

Reid, Francis *The Staging Handbook*, New York, 1978

UNITED STATES

It is impossible to give a comprehensive list of suppliers, and stockists in the space available. Those wishing to find a specific supplier should consult

Theatre Crafts Directory (P.O. Box 630 Holmes Pennsylvania PA 19043 – 9930.)

This publication gives comprehensive listings of suppliers for costume fabric, electrical supplies, dance-wear, curtains and drapes, film equipment, and flameproofing. It even lists about 50 suppliers of feathers for theatrical costumes!

Listed below are a representative selection of stockists and suppliers.

Costume, Props, Make-Up

Norcosto Inc.
3203 North Highway 100
Minneapolis
Minn. 55422
Tel: 612 533 2791

Stagecraft Industries
1302 Northwest Kearney Street
Portland
Oregon 97208
Tel: 503 226 7351

Theater Production Services
59 4th Avenue
New York
NY 10003
Tel: 914 941 0357

Tobins Lake Studios
2650 Seven Mile Road
South Lyon
Mich. 48178
Tel: 313 229 6666

Peter Wolf Associates Inc.
3800 Parry Avenue
Dallas
Texas 75226
Tel: 214 381 8000

Lighting and Sound

American Stage Lighting
Company
1331 C North Avenue
New Rochelle, NY 10804
Tel: 914 636 5538

Electro Controls
2975 South 2nd West Street
Salt Lake City
Utah 84115
Tel: 801 487 6111

Electronics Diversified
0625 S.W. Florida Street
Portland
Oregon 97219
Tel: 503 645 5533

General Electric Company
Lamp Department
Nela Park
Cleveland
Ohio 44112
Tel: 216 266 2121

Hub Electric Inc.
940 Industrial Drive
Elmhurst, Ill. 60126
Tel: 312 530 6860

Showco
9011 Governor's Row
Dallas
Texas 75247
Tel: 214 630 1188

Stage Equipment

Gothic Color Inc.
727 Washington Street
New York, NY 10014
Tel: 212 941 0977

Peter Albrecht Corporation
325 East Chicago Street
Milwaukee, Wis. 53202
Tel: 414 272 2811

SUPPLIERS AND STOCKISTS

UNITED KINGDOM

Listed below are a
representative selection of
suppliers and stockists.

**Costume, Props and
Make-Up**

Bapty and Co Ltd
703 Harrow Road
London NW10 – weapon hire
Tel: 01 969 6671

Bermans and Nathans
18 Irving Street
London WC2 – period costume:
Tel: 01 839 1651

Borovick Fabrics Ltd
16 Berwick Street
London WIV 4HP – theatrical
fabrics
Tel: 01 437 2180
Tel: 01 437 5020

Bristol Old Vic Hire
Colston Hall Vaults
Bristol BS1
Tel: 0272 701 026

Brodie and Middleton
68 Drury Lane
London WC2 – dyes, canvas,
metal powders and other paints
Tel: 01 836 3289

Freed Fredk Ltd
94 St Martin's Lane
London WC2 – theatrical shoes
Tel: 01 240 0432

Laurence Corner
62 Hampstead Road
London NW1 – period hats and
other unusual clothing
Tel: 01 388 6811

Old Times Furnishing Co
135 Lower Richmond Road
London SW15 – props, furniture
hire
Tel: 01 788 3551

Lighting and Sound

Ancient Lights
8 West Carr Road
Attleborough
Norfolk NR17 1AA – lighting

DHA Lighting Ltd
7 Bishops Terrace
Kennington
London SE11 – lighting
Tel: 01 582 3600

MAC (Sound Hire)
1 Attenbury Park Road
Altringham
Cheshire
WA14 5QE

Northern Stage Services Ltd
4 Beck Grove
Woodside
Shaw
Oldham OI2 8NG
Tel: 0706 849469

Rank Stand Ltd
P O Box 51
Great West Road
Brentford
Middlesex TW8 9HR – sound
Tel: 01 568 9222

Theatre Projects Services Ltd
8 Blundell Street
London N7 8BA
Tel: 01 609 2121

White Light (Electrics) Ltd
57 Filmer Road
London SW6
Tel: 01 731 3291

Stage Equipment

Furse Theatre Equipment
Traffic Street
Nottingham NG2
Tel: 0602 863 471

Northern Light
134 St Vincent Street
Glasgow G2 5JU
Tel: 041 440 1771

Rex Howard Drapes Ltd
Acton Park Industrial Estate
Eastman Road
The Vale
London W3
Tel: 01 749 5881

Theatre Flooring Ltd
Kent House
High Street
Farningham
DA4 0DT
Tel: 0322 865288

Theatre Project Services Ltd
14 Langley Street
London
WC2E 9LN
Tel: 01 240 5411

INDEX